About the author

Alex J. Bellamy is Professor of International Relations at The University of Queensland. His research focuses on the normative aspects of the use of military force, in particular the ethics and laws of war, peace operations and humanitarian intervention. His most recent books include *A Responsibility to Protect? The Global Effort Against Mass Killing, Just Wars: From Cicero to Iraq*, and (with Paul D. Williams and Stuart Griffin) *Understanding Peacekeeping.*

FIGHTING TERROR
Ethical dilemmas

Alex J. Bellamy

Zed Books
LONDON | NEW YORK

Fighting Terror: Ethical Dilemmas was first published in 2008 by
Zed Books Ltd, 7 Cynthia Street, London N1 9JF, UK and Room 400,
175 Fifth Avenue, New York, NY 10010, USA

www.zedbooks.co.uk

Set in Monotype Sabon and Gill Sans Heavy by Ewan Smith, London
Cover designed by Andrew Corbett
Printed and bound in Malta by Gutenberg Press Ltd

Distributed in the USA exclusively by Palgrave Macmillan, 175 Fifth
Avenue, New York, NY 10010, USA

A catalogue record for this book is available from the British Library
Library of Congress Cataloging in Publication Data available

ISBN 978 1 84277 967 5 hb
ISBN 978 1 84277 968 2 pb

Contents

Preface

In many ways, this book is a follow-on to my previous book on the just war tradition published in 2006 (*Just Wars: From Cicero to Iraq*).[1] My original intention was to use the just war tradition to evaluate the war on terror, among other matters, but space did not permit this. This book takes up and develops the moral framework set out in *Just Wars* as the basis for a systematic and thorough-going assessment of the war on terror. It substantially develops the arguments levelled in *Just Wars* about the nature of terrorism and the question of pre-emption and goes into much greater detail about the moral questions raised by these phenomena. It also substantially widens moral evaluation of the war on terror by exploring the importance of a moral understanding of war itself, evaluating whether the war on terror can be labelled a just war, the use of torture and moral questions about the sort of peace that the war will leave behind.

This book draws on five years of reflection on the ethics of the war on terror, and some of the ideas and arguments have been presented in earlier articles, though not in the systematic form offered here. The articles include 'International Law and the War in Iraq', *Melbourne Journal of International Law*, 4 (2), 2003; 'Ethics and Intervention: The "Humanitarian Exception" and the Problem of Abuse in the Case of Iraq', *Journal of Peace Research*, 41 (2), 2004; 'Supreme Emergencies and the Protection of Non-combatants in War', *International Affairs*, 80 (5), 2004; 'Is the War on Terror Just?', *International Relations*, 19 (3), 2005, pp. 275–96; 'No Pain, No Gain? Ethics and Torture in the War on Terror', *International Affairs*, 82 (1), 2006; 'Dirty Hands and Lesser Evils in the War on Terror', *British Journal of Politics and International Relations*, 9, 2007; 'Pre-empting Terror', in Alex J. Bellamy, Roland Bleiker, Sara E. Davies and Richard Devetak (eds), *Security and the War on Terror* (London: Routledge, 2007); and 'Torture, Terrorism and the Moral Prohibition on Killing Non-combatants', in W. G. Stritzke, S. Lewandowsky, D. Denemark, F. Morgan and J. Clare (eds), *Terrorism and Torture: An Interdisciplinary Perspective* (Cambridge: Cambridge University Press, 2008).

I am very grateful to Ellen McKinlay for her unfailing support for this project, as well as to Zed's anonymous reviewer. Thanks go to James Turner Johnson, James Muldoon, Richard Devetak, Richard Shapcott, Roland Bleiker, Cian O'Driscoll, Nicholas J. Wheeler and Paul D. Williams for helpful comments and advice on earlier versions of some of the chapters and related work.

Aptly enough, most of this book was written in the various libraries of UN agencies in Geneva. I am very grateful to the University of Queensland and the School of Political Science and International Studies for giving me the time away and financial support to do the reading, thinking and writing necessary to finish this book.

Finally, this book is dedicated to my darling wife Sara, who has walked with me every step of the way. She is a daily reminder of the things that are worth protecting. A gifted scholar, Sara has read and commented on every part of this book and challenged many of my ideas, forcing me back to the drawing board more than once. My best friend, she has provided immeasurable advice, support and help.

Note

1 Alex J. Bellamy, *Just Wars: From Cicero to Iraq* (Cambridge: Polity Press, 2006).

Introduction

The fall of the Berlin Wall has been replaced by 9/11 as the signpost for the contemporary era. Where once we described the times as 'post-Cold War', we now label them 'post-9/11' or the 'age of terror'. From this, overly simplistic, vantage point, the post-Cold War period was an interruption to world politics as usual, where liberalism reigned supreme without any serious ideological or material challenges. Then Al Qaeda launched an unprecedented wave of terror against New York and Washington, prompting the American government to respond with its era-defining 'war on terror'. The war on terror, such as it is, is a new kind of war, waged not against armies, states or nations, but against loose networks and well-hidden cells. It is a war without clearly defined goals. A war seemingly without victory or end.[1]

And yet it is not a war that one can simply dismiss out of hand as an immoral exercise of power. Our sensibilities tell us that there is something very wrong about Islamism, a doctrine that preaches hatred of others and advocates the extermination of men, women, children – soldiers and civilians alike – in pursuit of its eschatological goals. In the name of a chauvinist doctrine that shares much with Nazism, Islamist terrorists have shown themselves ready and willing to commit heinous wrongs. And what is more, they have attacked *our* civilians, *our* homes and *our* places of work, in America, Britain, Spain, Bali and elsewhere. Just as a world without Nazism is a better world for all, so too is a world without Islamic extremism.

We are therefore faced with a major moral dilemma, and it is the road we take that will define our contemporary era. From the Ancient Greek, a 'lemma' is a proposition that we hold to be true. A 'dilemma' occurs when we are forced to choose between two propositions (lemmas) that we hold to be true.[2] The dilemma that sits at the heart of this book is that on the one hand the world would be a better place and we would all be safer if there were no (or not many) Islamist terrorists, but on the other hand the use of force – which is sometimes tragically necessary to overcome violent and expansionist ideologies – can be ineffective and counter-productive. To put it in more specific terms, if I shoot a terrorist to prevent her killing civilians I might encourage her seven brothers to become terrorists. So how do I choose a course of action in the face of these two propositions that I believe to be true: (1) shooting the terrorist will prevent an attack and save civilians; (2) shooting the terrorist will create a martyr and encourage many others to become terrorists?

In this book I argue that in order to navigate this dilemma, and the many issue-specific dilemmas presented by the 'war on terror', we need moral anchorages. Moral anchorages should guide political decision-makers and the way that democratic societies debate and evaluate what is done in their name.[3] There are at least two important reasons why we need these moral anchorages, set out in more detail in Chapter 1. First of all, they tell us important things about who we are. We in the West are liberals and democrats. We believe in individual rights, open economies, free speech and due process. If we stop behaving according to our most dearly held principles, we cease to be who we are and become something less. If we do that, the terrorists win. Second, if it is anything at all, the war on terror is a war of ideas. Victory is not the complete absence of Islamist terrorism, but the rejection of Islamist terrorism by the global Islamic community. Victory is when the Islamists are marginalized in their own community. This victory may require the use of force to prevent individual attacks or deny terrorists the means to terrorize, but it cannot be won by force of arms alone. More importantly, force of arms not guided by moral anchorages, not constrained by *shared* expectations about appropriate behaviour, is counter-productive and will make it harder, not easier, to undermine Islamism.

I argue that a combination of principles drawn from the just war tradition and contemporary international law can provide us with the moral anchorages necessary to make good decisions about the type of war we want to fight. Together, these two sources combine distinctly Western, Christian and liberal ideas about using force with basic *shared* expectations regarding when and how force is employed and the responsibilities of belligerents afterwards. I begin in Chapter 1 by setting out the need for a moral framework in more detail and then defending a framework predicated on just war thinking and international law. To date, most prominent just war theorists have tended to defend certain aspects of the war on terror, including the invasion of Iraq.[4] In the chapters that follow, I take a much more critical approach and suggest that it is precisely our departure from shared moral principles that has contributed to the escalation of world terrorism and the mystique of Islamism. It is important to remember, however, that this shared moral framework categorically prohibits Islamist terrorism. Such terrorism can never be justified and can certainly provide grounds for the waging of just war upon it. That is the purpose of Chapter 2.

Nevertheless, the way we are fighting the war on terror falls significantly short of the moral mark. Specifically, I argue that although individual components might well be justified, the 'war on terror' as a whole cannot be considered just because it is too vague in its formulation, that pre-emptive self-defence can be employed only in specific sorts of circumstances, that torture is always wrong and that America and its allies have failed to fulfil their responsibilities to post-war Afghanistan and Iraq. There are alternative paths, and different routes are suggested in the chapters that follow. If, however, the use of force against Islamist terrorists is necessary in the future, it is imperative for it to be very obviously guided and constrained by shared moral principles. The price of not doing so will be paid in both an escalation of global terrorism and the erosion of the very values we are fighting to defend.

ONE
Ethics and war: an oxymoron?

Are ethics in war possible? Are they desirable? What sort of ethical framework should we use? To begin answering these questions, it is worth surveying arguments *against* ethical thinking in war. There are four broad arguments. The first two cast doubt on whether ethics can be applied to war in general, while the latter two insist only that ethical concerns do not apply to the war on terror. They are:

- the 'realist' argument that morality should not constrain what nations are entitled to do to defend themselves;
- the pacifist argument that all war is immoral;
- the 'neoconservative' argument that a war on terror is self-evidently just and that critical ethical scrutiny of its conduct implies sympathy for the terrorists;
- the 'reciprocity' argument that we should show moral and legal courtesies only to those who afford them to us.

On closer scrutiny, there are serious moral and practical problems with all four positions.

Realism

The argument that ethics have no role to play in war is most often associated with the 'realist' school, whose adherents include US Secretary of State Condoleezza Rice (at least before she became Secretary of State) and former National Security Advisor Henry Kissinger. For the realist, the state has two main purposes: to ensure its own survival and to enable the community it protects to live according to its own ideas about the good life. This translates into a disarmingly simple agenda for government. Governments are responsible for securing the national interest. In foreign policy, they operate in a world devoid of ethics in which policy outcomes are determined by the distribution and effective application of power.

From this perspective, the ethics of waging a war on terror are inconsequential. What matters is what will work to prevent future attacks. If, for example, torturing suspected terrorists will elicit information and deter other terrorists, then torture is legitimate. If 'regime change' is the only way of guaranteeing that a particular government will not assist terrorists in the production of weapons of mass destruction (WMD), then that too is legitimate. The realist message for the war on terror, therefore, seems clear enough. A logic that has permeated US strategic thinking since September 11 is that the state must be free to make its own decisions about the best way to defend itself. For example, after an Israeli attack on what it claimed were terrorist training camps inside Syria, George W. Bush told the world that 'Israel *must not feel constrained* in terms of defending the homeland'.[1] The basic idea is that defence of the state and its citizens is a good in itself and requires no further justification. Abstract moral rules should be sacrificed to guarantee success at as minimal a cost as possible.

In terms of how we should fight, the realist points us to the words of the American Civil War General, William T. Sherman, who famously declared that 'war is hell'.[2] Sherman contended that war could not be made humane through the application of law or morality and that those fighting with right on their side were entitled to use any measure necessary for victory. All blame for the suffering caused by war should rest with those whose wrongdoings made war necessary in the first place.[3]

In the war on terror, the US and its allies have sometimes made precisely this argument to justify the inadvertent but foreseeable killing of civilians. A common refrain among government officials is that the coalition of the willing bears no responsibility for non-combatant deaths. Instead, responsibility was said to lie squarely with Al Qaeda, the Taliban and Saddam Hussein's regime. Tony Blair, for instance, told the Iraqi people that 'our enemy is not you but your barbarous rulers', insisting that the suffering endured by ordinary Iraqis was caused by their former government's actions, not those of the invaders.[4]

It is here, though, that matters get complicated. Classical realism, understood as a broad tradition with its roots in Thucydides' account of warfare in ancient Greece[5] and Machiavelli's advice to the Medici princes of Renaissance Italy,[6] is deeply infused with a moral tone that contains some chilling lessons for those who believe that the powerful can act without concern for others. These writers taught us that states should avoid imposing their own moral preferences on others because this only instils resistance; that breaking commonly agreed moral rules encourages others to unite in opposition; that power is much more effective when it is exercised with consent – that is, when it is widely seen as legitimate; that war, as Carl von Clausewitz explained in the nineteenth century,[7] is an uncertain and unpredictable policy tool that should be used sparingly to achieve specific policy outcomes. These insights partly explain why many recent realists have criticized their country's wars. For example, Hans Morgenthau, the doyen of post-war realism, opposed America's intervention in Vietnam; more recently, prominent realists John Mearsheimer and Stephen Walt argued against the 2003 invasion of Iraq.[8]

Besides the fact that today's 'realists' have evidently done a poor job of representing their own intellectual tradition, there are a number of other serious problems with their propositions.

First, by disregarding standards of behaviour that have taken decades if not centuries to evolve, they risk undermining the basic rules of behaviour that underpin international order. The power of these constraints, such as the ban on the use of force contained in the UN Charter – a ban which has, incidentally, presided over a marked and steady decrease in the occurrence and lethality of war in the past sixty years – derive from their incorporation into customary practice. In the fifth century BC, the Athenian decision to break the customs of war to further its own interests led to the complete erosion of those customs, to the long-term detriment of both the Athenian empire and Greek civilization as a whole. As war between Greek *poleis* (city states) became more violent, so Greek civilization was weakened from within, leaving it unable to defend itself against Persian and Roman colonists.[9]

Second, unjust behaviour in the name of necessity encourages our adversaries to use similar tactics and leaves us without a common moral language to evaluate the justness or otherwise of such actions. If we consider it legitimate to breach moral rules to further our own cause, we have to acknowledge that our opponents may do likewise, a theme I will return to later.

This brings us to the third objection: war conduct perceived to be unjust would make it more difficult to negotiate a just end to the war and build a self-sustaining peace afterwards. Writing at the end of the eighteenth century, Immanuel Kant argued that it was important not to wage unlimited war, because doing so would make it very difficult to create a just and enduring peace and would in all likelihood sow the seeds of future war by creating a groundswell of resentment and hostility.[10] This is particularly pertinent for the war on terror, because victory depends on our undermining popular support for Al Qaeda.

The final objection turns our gaze inwards. The whole purpose of fighting a war is to protect core values that we hold dear. It simply makes no sense to wage a war to protect core values in a way that erodes those very values. Perhaps the most basic of liberal values is the idea that it is wrong to kill or otherwise harm the innocent. Michael Ignatieff describes this supposition as a 'pre-political' commitment – it is a necessary precondition for liberal politics that individuals be free from arbitrary harm.[11] The realists would have us dispose of this commitment if short-term interests appeared to dictate. But as Christopher Coker recently argued, we cannot do away with, ignore or even override our basic liberal values without ceasing to be liberals.[12] Any 'victory' achieved by sacrificing our most basic values would be a hollow one at best.

Pacifism

A second type of response to September 11 is to reaffirm the belief that the phrase 'ethics of war' is an oxymoron because war is always unjust. Two similar yet distinctive means of doing this have been developed. 'Deontological' pacifists argue that killing is intrinsically wrong and that there are no situations, real or imaginary, in which resort to war would be a lesser evil. Others propose a form of 'consequentialist' pacifism and argue that although there may be imaginary circumstances in which war may be the lesser evil, it is highly unlikely that any war could be deemed justifiable. For both types, not only is the war on terror unjust, but moral scrutiny is dangerous because it offers a language which skilful policy-makers can use to justify their violent deeds, unintentionally helping to humanize and thereby legitimize the practice of war itself.

One of the most sophisticated writers in this genre is Richard Holmes, who blends deontological and consequentialist forms of pacifism. Holmes rejects the deontological position that killing is wrong per se because it may in some circumstances be quite right to kill those who are guilty of, or in the process of committing, heinous crimes. However, we all agree that killing the innocent is wrong. Although the ethics and laws of war prohibit the deliberate killing of non-combatants, in reality the innocent are always killed in war and are likely to be so for the foreseeable future. Thus Holmes combines the deontological prescription, accepted by most people, that non-combatants may not be deliberately killed, with the consequentialist observation that non-combatants are always killed in war.[13] Only when political and military leaders can guarantee that no non-combatants will die might wars be considered legitimate. Clearly, the war on terror failed this test, probably on day one. As such, no further moral scrutiny is required.

This argument should give us all pause for thought. It is not one that can easily be dismissed without doing a disservice to our basic sensibilities. For all its sophistication, however, it is a moral theory based on how we would like the world to be, not on how it actually is. In essence, it calls upon governments to abrogate the moral responsibility to protect their citizens in order to uphold a higher moral good, despite the fact that there is no universal agreement about the nature of that good. This reflects the position of the earliest Christians who, expecting the imminent return of Christ, removed themselves from public life and adopted a pacifist view on violence. This position became increasingly untenable as the 'second coming' became more remote and even more so after the conversion of Constantine brought Christianity into public life. Gradually, many Christians assumed public office and abandoned pacifism.

Those in public office have a moral responsibility to protect the wider community. In the absence of a world government or commonly adhered-to rules prohibiting organized violence, endangering the lives of citizens to satisfy one's own moral predilections by prima facie rejecting the use of force in the face of threats is to abrogate the responsibilities of government, undermine the legitimacy of the polity, and thereby behave immorally.

Both realism and pacifism are therefore unsatisfactory starting points. However, if there are certain elements of realism that our moral exploration of the war on terror needs to bear in mind – especially the moral responsibilities of governments, the idea of military necessity and the principle of prudence – the presumption against violence that lies at the heart of pacifism should be included in our assessment, not least because it grows out of the basic idea that it is wrong to kill the innocent. This is a proposition I will defend at greater length in the following chapter, because it is precisely the intention to kill non-combatants that marks terrorism out as a form of violence and explains why it elicits the sort of moral outrage that it (quite rightly) does.

Neoconservatism

Neoconservatism began life as a liberal reaction against opposition to the Vietnam War in the mid-1960s. Liberals such as Irving Kristol believed that the war's critics were either too eager to sacrifice the South Vietnamese people to communist tyranny in order to save American lives and dollars, or else were simply blinded by their ideological preference for leftist politics. In contrast to liberal defeatism, the neoconservatives saw the struggle as one between good and evil in a world of black and white moral certainties that was given philosophical voice by Leo Strauss. In 1997, the neoconservatives set out their political stall by setting up the *Project for the New American Century* to counter what they saw as the 'incoherent' and morally bankrupt policies of the Clinton administration. The *Project* called for increased defence spending to enable an aggressive policy of maintaining American hegemony, spreading democracy and confronting 'evil'. It argued that America's democratic purpose and material power gave it special responsibilities to promote democracy and confront tyranny everywhere. What is more, neoconservatives argued that it was 'empirical fact' not 'American exceptionalism' that gave America responsibility (and hence special rights) for leadership in the war on terrorism.[14]

With the advent of George W. Bush, a number of prominent neoconservatives, including Dick Cheney, Donald Rumsfeld and Paul Wolfowitz, came into government and helped shape America's response to Al Qaeda. The ideology's black-and-white view of the world was clearly evident in Bush's post-9/11 challenge to the world: you are either 'with us' or 'against us'. Neoconservatism gave the war on terror its overarching justification. It would be more than simply a war of self-defence against a relatively small group of Afghan-based radicals. Instead, as Natan Sharansky of the American Enterprise Institute put it:

> We are in the midst of the first world war of the twenty-first century, waged between the world of terror and the world of democracy, between a civilization in which human life is held in the highest value and one for which human life is merely an instrument to reach certain political aims. The world of democracy will win this struggle. But in order for the victory to be everlasting, it is crucial, but not sufficient, to destroy the terror. It is imperative to expand the world our enemies try to destroy, to export democracy.[15]

Neoconservatives therefore believe that the military effort against terrorists and their supporters is inherently just. Indeed, so just is this cause that it cannot be inhibited by international laws or moral rules. During the Vietnam War, they argued that the war's critics confused 'means' and 'ends', and tended to ignore the latter entirely. If it was right to save the Vietnamese from communist tyranny, then it must be right – they argued – to do whatever was necessary to prevail. Alvin Friedman, the Deputy Assistant Secretary for Defense under Lyndon Johnson, expressed it neatly when he asked in 1966: 'what do we mean by ethics in war? It is a war to which there is no alternative if we are going to defend the ultimate values.' In such a war, there is no tension between what is right and what is necessary, because one must do whatever is necessary in order to do good. Thus, 'do we sacrifice moral ends in our insistence on moral means? What *are* moral means in view of the fact that any means adopted are presumably in pursuit of a moral goal?'[16]

This basic argument, that the moral ends justify the means, has been used to justify various components of the war on terror. In America, everything from unauthorized wire-tapping to detention declared unlawful by the Supreme Court has been justified by reference to the moral ends – the defeat of terrorism. Globally, assassinations, missile attacks, torture and much more has been justified in this way. Even to question this logic is to attract withering criticism.

Because this logic has guided much of the moral defence of individual aspects of the war on terror, I will return to neoconservatism later. At this stage, however, it is worth noting three general problems. Firstly, and most importantly, although it rails against pluralism and postmodernism and in favour of moral certitudes, neoconservatism is itself a form of moral relativism. In essence, its ethics boil down to, 'X is right because it is what I believe to be right'. It is premised on the belief that, given the opportunity, individuals everywhere would choose to be *homo economicus*: rational, self-centred and materialist individuals driven by the same concerns and desires that drive ordinary Americans.[17] The neoconservatives reject the need for moral debate or consensus because they are so certain that they are right.

The second problem relates to the standing of these moral certainties in world politics. When translated into foreign policy, neoconservativism fails one of the first tests of realism. Reflecting on the failure of the League of Nations shortly before the Second World War, the British historian E. H. Carr delivered a withering 'realist' attack on the utopian sentiments at the League's heart. What the League's founders failed to remember, Carr argued, is that what they believed were 'universal values' (such as self-determination, the Versailles territorial settlement and minority rights) were actually merely the interests of the powerful cloaked in the veneer of morality. Failing to appreciate this, the League's primary sponsors, Britain and France, could not understand that other emerging powers – in particular the fascist powers – might believe the system to be unjust. Believing their interests to be identical with the common good, Britain and France did not try to fashion a world order acceptable to all the world's powerful actors. The resulting order, viewed as inherently unjust by a few powerful actors, was ultimately doomed to fail.[18] A parochial and distinctly American view of the world, which grants an unlimited moral licence for American interference in the affairs of others, neoconservatism mistakenly assumes that what is good for America must be good for the world. Indeed the *Project for the New American Century* explicitly says as much. This is to make the mistake of believing that one's particular view of the world is universal. Carr ably set out the dangers associated with this path nearly seventy years ago.

Finally, while the spreading of democracy is a core component of neoconservatism, the neoconservatives themselves are rather sketchy on how this might actually be done. Beyond arguing that it may occasionally be necessary to use violence to overthrow tyrants and terrorists, neoconservatives have tended to avoid thorny questions about how democracy spreads and takes root. At the most abstract level, this is a problem derived from neoconservativism's black-and-white view of the world, which makes it hard to see how it can persuade those of different moral viewpoints or build consensus around its ideals. Writing in the nineteenth century, John Stuart Mill argued that oppressed people themselves should overthrow their oppressors because democracy built by outsiders was unlikely to take root.[19] While critics of this view point to Germany and Japan as cases of successful externally driven democratization, contemporary Afghanistan and Iraq provide a somewhat more sobering perspective.

Reciprocity

The fourth perspective holds that ethical and legal restraints are embedded in reciprocal social relations. Because jihadist terrorists reject those restraints, deliberately violate their core precepts and seek to exploit the moral restraints observed by their opponents, those waging a war on terror are freed from moral obligation towards them and their supporters. Indeed, some writers have taken this even further, arguing that reciprocity is impossible in the war on terror because Islam has nothing analogous to the principle of non-combatant immunity.[20] As an aside, this position is quite incorrect – there is, in fact, a strong tradition of Islamic law in relation to non-combatant immunity that mirrors rather closely that of the West's just war tradition.[21]

The basic idea of reciprocity is as old as the legal and moral regulation of war itself. Ancient Greek polities observed reciprocal codes of conduct in wars with each other, but not in wars with Persians, because reciprocity was not possible across such deep civilizational divides.

The principle of reciprocity underpins the contemporary laws of war. When Britain signed the first Protocol to the 1949 Geneva Conventions, it issued a reservation permitting itself to use measured reprisals if the enemy engaged in deliberate attacks on civilians.[22] Nor is this argument without legal merit. Although the Geneva Conventions grant everyone the right to be treated humanely in Common Article 3, they reserve the rights of full belligerency to armed organizations that display insignia and whose soldiers carry arms openly and abide by the Conventions. Because today's jihadist terrorists do none of these things, the law says that they deserve only the basic minimum right to be treated humanely. The moral case expands this logic and suggests that because terrorists reject the rules, those fighting terrorists are also freed of their obligations to follow them. As Steven Forde put it before September 11, the basic proposition of this perspective is that, 'acting in accordance with the international common good when others refuse to do so is harmful, and perhaps even immoral, considering the state's obligation to the safety of its members'.[23]

The question of reciprocity has been most prominent in relation to the use of torture against Al Qaeda suspects and the indefinite detention of individuals at Guantánamo Bay and elsewhere. As this is the topic of Chapter 5, here I will limit myself to demonstrating briefly the form this argument takes. Successive Attorneys General in the US have made the reciprocity argument in order to create a permissive legal environment for torture. John Ashcroft (2001–05) lambasted human rights activists who complained about the mistreatment of prisoners, arguing that granting rights to terrorists only helped them. He warned, 'to those who scare peace-loving people with phantoms of lost liberty; my message is this: your tactics only aid terrorists'.[24] His successor, Alberto Gonzales, wrote a memorandum to the President on 25 January 2002 in which he argued that:

> the nature of the new war [on terrorism] places a high premium
> on other factors, such as the ability to quickly obtain information

from captured terrorists and their sponsors in order to avoid further atrocities against American civilians ... This new paradigm renders obsolete Geneva's [the 1949 Geneva Protocol on the Treatment of Prisoners of War] strict limitations on questioning of enemy prisoners.[25]

What is wrong with this argument? First of all, the non-reciprocity argument does not release us from our legal obligations. Irrespective of what we might think of terrorists, we have a legal obligation under the Geneva Conventions to treat all individuals 'humanely'. There is also a whole host of legal conventions forbidding the use of torture or cruel and degrading treatment, the deliberate targeting of non-combatants and assassination. None of these legal conventions rests on reciprocity. In other words, we are legally obliged to obey these rules irrespective of what our enemy does.

But what about the moral component? Is it not wrong (not to say imprudent) to fight a great evil with one hand tied behind your back? It is indeed important to win just wars, but I do not know of a case where a state fighting a just war lost *because* it fought according to the moral rules of the day. Nor are there clear cases of states securing decisive advantages by breaking the rules. The most often talked about case in this regard is the RAF's terror bombing of German cities in the Second World War. If the deliberate killing of German civilians was necessary to end the war and its attendant Holocaust, was that then the right thing to do? The simplest response to this is to point out that, according to the US Strategic Bombing Survey conducted after the war, the terror bombing of German cities played almost no part in defeating Germany. Despite the bombing, German war production was higher at the end of the war than it was at the beginning. At war's end, Germany still had two million men under arms and tens of thousands of tanks, artillery pieces and other war-making material. What brought Germany to its knees was not the indiscriminate terror bombing, but the precise and steady destruction of its oil stocks, conducted mainly by the American air force.[26] But what if the bombing had been instrumental in defeating Germany? In such cases are we obliged to obey the rules and risk defeat?

Liberal societies expect their leaders and their militaries to follow the basic moral and legal rules even when their adversaries do not. Opinion polls taken in Britain during the Second World War show that even after the Blitz, there was never a majority of Britons favouring terror attacks on Germany. There are at least two reasons for this. First, although law – especially international law – might be reciprocal, morality typically is not. Unless one subscribes entirely to a consequentialist ethics, and very few humans do, acts such as murder, rape and child pornography remain immoral irrespective of what others do to each other or, for that matter, to us. Second, we need to reiterate an earlier point: that fighting and sacrificing to protect something is morally sensible only if that something is worth protecting. If we sacrifice what is good about the thing we are protecting in order to protect it, we lose the moral purpose behind defending it in the first place. Above all, it is vital in war to avoid becoming the very thing we are fighting. In a letter to his son Christopher in 1944, J. R. R. Tolkien wrote:

> there was a solemn article in the local paper seriously advocating systematic exterminating of the entire German nation as the only proper course after military victory: because, if you please, they are rattlesnakes, and don't know the difference between good and evil! (What of the writer?) The Germans have just as much right to declare the Poles and Jews exterminable vermin, subhuman, as we have to select the Germans. Of course, there is a difference here. The article was answered, and the answer printed … *You can't fight the Enemy with his own Ring without turning into an Enemy.*[27]

If we wage war to right a wrong, but commit similar wrongs in the process or erode some of the very ideas we purport to be fighting for – perhaps because the enemy refuses to obey the rules – then we risk doing as much damage to ourselves as to our enemy. One cannot defend 'democracy' and 'freedom' by detaining people without trial, killing non-combatants, overriding the rule of law and undermining 'pre-political' commitments that enable democratic politics. Doing so limits our enjoyment of these rights and risks devaluing the moral standing of terms such as 'democracy' and 'freedom' themselves.

The value of ethics

From the preceding discussion, it seems clear that any engagement with the war on terror needs to take ethics seriously. Whether they are recognized as such or not, moral questions sit at the heart of all political and strategic debates concerning war. Although ethics are often obscured, masked by the veneer of realism, pacifism, the relativism of neoconservativism or the formalism of non-reciprocity, morality is constantly working to justify or challenge certain elements of war. But these four attempts to limit the scope of moral scrutiny are all flawed. What we need instead is an explicit moral framework.

For the reasons set out above, it is always important to think seriously about the ethical presuppositions that guide our actions, especially in war. When fighting terror, this need is heightened because this war is first and foremost a war of ideas and one that can be won only if a significant portion of humanity comes to believe that jihadist terrorism is wrong and the measures taken to deal with the threat they pose. None of the four perspectives set out above is capable of articulating a strategy for winning the war on terror. Of the four, the pacifist alternative would be likely to do least damage. This is because, alongside measures to disrupt the terrorists and prevent specific attacks, in the long term the only viable strategy for defeating Al Qaeda is to undermine its popular support. This can be done only if the measures we take against Al Qaeda are understood as legitimate in key parts of the world.

In 2006, Audrey Kurth Cronin[28] identified seven ways in which, historically, non-state terrorism has been brought to an end or into decline.[29] They are:

1 Capturing or killing the leader (e.g. Shining Path, Real IRA).
2 Failure to transition to next generation (e.g. Red Brigades).
3 Achievement of the group's aims (e.g. Irgun, ANC).
4 Transition to a legitimate political process (e.g. IRA, PLO).
5 Undermining of popular support (e.g. ETA).
6 Repression (e.g. PKK, People's Will).
7 Transition from terrorism to other forms of violence, notably criminality and insurgency (e.g. Abu Sayyaf, FARC).

These factors are not mutually exclusive.

Which of these approaches holds most promise for the war against Al Qaeda and its allies? Helpfully, Paul Williams has looked at this question. Given the fact that Al Qaeda is a loose network and many, if not most, of its cells are more or less self-forming and self-reliant, Williams argues that killing or arresting the leadership is unlikely to have much effect. Indeed, the Iraq insurgency demonstrates this only too well. Key insurgency leaders have been arrested and killed without any noticeable impact on the pattern of violence. It is equally unlikely that Al Qaeda will fail to manage 'generational change', not least because it appears to have no shortage of young people willing to fight in its campaigns. Being a loose network, Al Qaeda has also successfully 'piggy-backed' on to local conflicts in Kashmir, Algeria, Somalia, Chechnya and the Philippines.

Nor is it likely, Williams argues (thankfully), that Al Qaeda will achieve its objectives. It seeks to remove all governments within the land of Islam that do not rule according to its fundamentalist interpretation of the faith. According to bin Laden, Western influence in the Islamic world has corrupted and divided the region's governments, making Muslims subservient to the West. Al Qaeda aims to overthrow these corrupt governments and replace them with a unified Islamic state – a caliphate. It also wishes to end what it sees as the American oppression of Muslims worldwide. But by all accounts, it enjoys the direct support of only a minority in the Islamic world. After all, the Taliban experience in Afghanistan suggests that the proposed caliphate would be much *more* oppressive than the prevailing status quo. However, and this is where things get complicated and where it becomes clear that the war on terror coalition is walking on a fine tightrope, although Al Qaeda is not widely supported in the Muslim world, not least because the overwhelming majority of Muslims reject its brand of fundamentalism and are not prepared to follow the path of violence, it is widely respected both for standing up to the West and for its members' devotion to the faith.[30] Nevertheless, Al Qaeda lacks the support it needs to realize its political goals and so is unlikely to make the transition to a legitimate political process. After all, it staunchly denies the legitimacy of almost every political figure in the Muslim world.

Williams argues that evidence from the past six years of waging a war on terror suggests that option 6, repression, is also unlikely to work. Despite an annual defence budget of $500 billion, the invasion and occupation of Iraq and Afghanistan, the use of air power against Yemen and Somalia and the incarceration of thousands of suspected terrorists around the world, the war on terror has failed to stem the tide of Al Qaeda-inspired terrorism. The possible reasons are well recognized in defence circles. Al Qaeda is a virtual network that has little central command and direction. Its diffuse cells are barely connected to one another and operate for long periods in isolation. The network is global in reach and able to shift rapidly to hide itself and take advantage of weaknesses wherever they appear. It is also virtual in that it uses the internet for recruitment, propaganda, fundraising and planning. This process accelerated after Al Qaeda lost its base in Afghanistan. Of course, there are things that counter-terrorism agencies can do to disrupt these networks. They can disrupt funds, interdict supplies and people, wage war online, and use force to prevent individual cells from actualizing their terrorist ambitions, but they cannot strike a decisive military blow. Repression, therefore, is unlikely.

This, according to Williams, leaves options 5 and 7: undermine Al Qaeda's support base or help to engineer a transition from terrorism to other forms of violence. In relation to the latter, Al Qaeda is already transitioning to both criminality and insurgency. As Williams points out, it is engaged in a web of criminal activity designed to fund its terrorist activities. This opens an opportunity to attack the organization by taking measures to cut its supply of funds but, for the reasons set out above, it is unlikely that this strategy alone would be decisive.

Another alternative is to encourage Al Qaeda to replace terrorism with insurgency, then insurgency with regular war. In other words, allow it to develop the sorts of traditional military capabilities that would permit the West to engage it in a 'fair' conventional fight where a decisive blow might be struck. This has occasionally happened in the past. US forces in Indochina fared much better after the Tet offensive required the Vietcong to rely more heavily on the conventional North Vietnamese army. But this scenario is unlikely and deeply problematic. Al Qaeda knows that it would not last long if it became a conventional force – the fate of the Taliban and Saddam Hussein provide ample warning of this. It also believes that time is on its side – that it can prevail if it can outlast the US. This is a lesson it draws from Vietnam and from its own experience with the Soviet Union in Afghanistan. In addition, the bloody nose that Hezbollah gave to Israel in 2006, the resurgence of insurgency in Afghanistan and its persistence in Iraq all suggest that diffuse and low-level violence is the best way to fight the American superpower.

We are therefore left agreeing with Paul Williams that, although military measures may have their place in disrupting terror networks, negating their supply of funds and arms, preventing them acquiring WMD and state sponsors, aiding frontline states and preventing specific terror attacks, only option 5 – undermining the organization's popular support – will deliver victory. How, precisely, one goes about doing this is well beyond the scope of this book. The key point for us is that the way in which the war on terror is conducted must at the very least avoid undermining this goal and should aim to contribute to it. The only way we will do this is if people – particularly people within Al Qaeda's constituency – believe that the way we apply military force is legitimate, just, discriminating, proportionate and compassionate. Every time we fail to live up to these standards, we make it harder to undermine popular support for Al Qaeda and we reduce our chances of victory.

This has been a long way round at getting to the crucial point – *we cannot win the war on terror unless we conduct it in a manner that is commonly seen as legitimate.* Ethics in war are never an optional extra, and in this war they are essential to victory. Moreover, persuading ourselves of the legitimacy of what we do is only one small part of the exercise. We also need to persuade Al Qaeda's potential constituency. To do that we need high standards and a common moral language.

What type of ethics?

In the West at least, there is a reasonably broad consensus that the most appropriate ethical framework for evaluating war is the just war tradition. This tradition has its roots in Roman law, was

developed by early Christian theologians such as St Ambrose and
St Augustine, became part of the Church's law (Canon Law) during
the Middle Ages, and was then gradually secularized by the jurists
of the Renaissance and Enlightenment, especially Gentili, Grotius
and Vattel. Today, it underpins the laws of war agreed to by states of
all stripes. In its present form, the just war tradition can be divided
into two sets of moral requirements: *jus ad bellum* requirements
about the reasons for waging war, and *jus in bello* rules governing
how wars ought to be fought. Recently, a third set of principles
relating to how the victors should conduct themselves after the war
has been developed (*jus post bellum*). This is discussed in greater
detail in Chapter 6.[31]

Jus ad bellum comprises three types of criteria: substantive, prudential and procedural. There are four substantive criteria. The
first is right intention: individuals must wage war for the common
good, not out of hatred or for self-aggrandizement. According to
the tradition's early theologians, killing for personal gain or because
of hatred or envy is sinful. When a soldier kills another, therefore,
he must do so only because it is necessary to defend the common
good or right a wrong.

The second substantive rule is that war may be waged only for a
just cause. This is usually limited to self-defence, defence of others,
restoration of peace, defence of rights and the punishment of wrongdoers. Just cause is often viewed in absolute terms: a combatant
either has a just cause or does not, a view that sits comfortably
with a legalist perspective which holds that actors either comply
with the law or violate it.[32] However, from the time of Francisco
de Vitoria in the sixteenth century, just war writers have tended
to separate 'objective' or 'true justice' (knowable to God) from
'subjective' justice (knowable to humans). To we humans, wars can
certainly *appear* just on both sides because we are unable to take a
'God's eye' view of the matter. There are two ways of coping with
this. First, as Vitoria argued, leaders should take care to make sure
that their grounds for war are solid by seeking advice from learned
people and listening to the arguments of others. This they should
do in good faith. Second, the just cause rule should be understood

in relative terms. Thus, it is not a matter of either having or not having a just cause, but of having more or less of one.

This leads us to the third substantive *jus ad bellum* criterion: proportionality of ends. This asks whether the overall harm likely to be caused by war is less than that caused by the wrong that is being righted. Vitoria suggested that proportionality plays a significant role in judgements about the legitimacy of war: while war was legitimate to right wrongs, not all wrongs legitimized war. Some wrongs are simply not serious enough to justify the inevitable evils involved in waging war.

The final substantive test is last resort: is the use of force the only, or most proportionate, way that the wrong is likely to be righted? Last resort does not require the exhaustion of every means short of force. If it did, force would never be licit because there is always an alternative to fighting (such as subjugation or death). Last resort demands that actors carefully evaluate all the different strategies that might bring about the desired end, selecting force only if it appears to be the most feasible and proportionate one.

Jus ad bellum's prudential criteria impose important checks on decisions to wage what would otherwise be justifiable wars. The principal rule in this regard is reasonable chance of success. This criterion insists that because war always entails some degree of evil, it is wrong to use violence unless we can reasonably expect to prevail.

The third type of criterion is the procedural requirements of right authority and proper declaration. Only political leaders with no legal superior are entitled to authorize war. After the seventeenth century this translated into sovereign states, and from the eighteenth until the mid-twentieth centuries states were effectively given a free hand to authorize war whenever they saw fit. This right was heavily restricted, however, by the 1945 UN Charter. The question of who has the right to authorize war remains a moot point today. International law suggests that only states under attack and the UN Security Council have this right. Many moralists, however, argue that individual states and coalitions may legitimately wage war in other instances. Furthermore, it is widely accepted today that other actors – such as national liberation movements – may also legitimately wage war in some circumstances, a question I will address in greater detail in the following chapter. For now, we should remember that the concern underpinning discussion of rightful authority is that force be used for the common good and not for selfish purposes.

The requirement for proper declaration had its origins in the Roman *fetial* system, which set out procedures for declaring war. During the Middle Ages, the declaration requirement supported the right authority test because only those princes with the authority to declare war and not be removed from power had the right to wage war. The requirement also forced those about to embark on war to state their case, providing an opportunity for peaceful restitution. Nowadays, the declaration can serve a third purpose: it clearly marks the transition from peace to war and hence the type of rules that ought to be applied. The problem is that a declaration of 'permanent war', such as the war on terror, creates deep ambiguity about what standards should apply.

Jus in bello regulates the conduct of war. It contains three basic rules. First, the principle of discrimination: non-combatants must never be deliberately attacked. Second, the principle of proportionality: military targets may be attacked only when their military value outweighs the foreseeable destruction that will result. Third, combatants must not use prohibited weapons or conduct themselves in ways that violate the laws of war.

Underpinning *jus in bello* is the doctrine of double-effect, first articulated by St Thomas Aquinas in the fourteenth century. According to Aquinas, any act may have two consequences: one that is intended and one that is not. Even if we intend good, our actions might cause unintended negative consequences. Unintended negative consequences are excusable if four conditions are satisfied:

1 The desired end must be good in itself.
2 Only the good effect is intended.
3 The good effect must not be produced by means of the evil effect.
4 The good of the good effect must outweigh the evil of the evil effect (proportionality).[33]

However, when applied to civilian casualties of war, there is a major flaw with this account. As Michael Walzer explains:

> Simply not to intend the death of civilians is too easy ... What we look for in such cases is some sign of a positive commitment to save civilian lives. Not merely to apply the proportionality rule and kill no more civilians than is militarily necessary ... Civilians have a right to something more. And if saving civilian lives means risking soldiers' lives, the risk must be accepted.[34]

There is a powerful argument that in practice there is no difference between *intending* the deaths of non-combatants and merely *foreseeing* them. If you foresee something evil happening as a result of something you do, yet you do it anyway, how can it be said that you did not intend that evil? This is a particularly acute problem in the war on terror, where victory depends on perception. To put it bluntly, when children and other civilians are killed in air raids, it does not matter to the victims, their relatives and the wider community whether the bombing was deliberate or accidental. Double-effect might assure us that what we do is moral, but that is not enough. We need a higher standard.

According to Walzer and, it should be said, international law, we can ascertain something approximating intentions by focusing on what people actually do. To display an intention not to harm non-combatants, we must demonstrate that we have taken every reasonable precaution to minimize the likelihood of harming non-combatants. This is the principle of 'due care'. Combatants must take active precautions to prevent the accidental killing of non-combatants even if that means increasing the risk to themselves – though how much risk they must accept is a moot point.

Above all, the just war tradition provides a common vocabulary by which to argue about war and make moral judgements. Much of that vocabulary is nowadays used and understood outside of the West. However, we must avoid the temptation of thinking that all we have to do is 'apply' the criteria to the war on terror in order to make definitive moral judgements. There are two problems with this way of approaching things. First, it overlooks the fact that people working with the same moral vocabulary can reach very different conclusions about how these principles apply in practice. Second, there is a danger of falling into the sort of moral relativism espoused by the neoconservatives. That is, I might persuade myself of the justness of my cause and appeal to the just war tradition as a source of authority. Having done so, I can argue that those who disagree with me are either applying the just war framework in a 'defective' fashion or are allowing politics and ideology to skew their moral compass. Sadly, much contemporary just war thinking about the war on terror falls into this trap.[35]

These traits also have direct and deeply problematic consequences for the way we think about and prosecute the war on terror. Most pointedly, having used a Christian-based moral tradition to persuade ourselves of the justice of our cause and the moral superiority of the way we fight, we cease to scrutinize the way we act and, more importantly, the way that others perceive us. So, for example, if we use just war reasoning to argue that the Iraq invasion was just, and if the overwhelming majority of humanity disagrees with us, we can account for that disparity only in one of four ways. They either operate with imperfect moral frameworks, apply a defective account of our moral framework, simply misunderstand the facts or support the commission of evil. The problem, of course, is that used in this way the just war tradition ceases to be a common moral vocabulary. Instead it becomes exactly what critics from Erasmus onwards have charged: a casuist's tool for justifying war and the exercise of power. Such a tradition can play no part in guiding policies to combat jihadist terrorism in such a way as to undermine popular support for it. On the contrary, it would only serve to widen the gap between what 'we' think is legitimate and what much of the rest of the world thinks is legitimate. This would leave us perplexed about why so many people hate us when, by our way of thinking, all we do is good. It is not surprising that in the past five years, many of our political leaders have expressed precisely this sort of confusion.

Clearly, if we want to use the vocabulary of just war we need to set out some parameters for applying it and adjudicating disputes. I propose two parameters that I will refer to again and again. The first points to the importance of consensus; the second stresses universality and consistency.

The first parameter refers to the nature of ethics itself. 'Ethics' reside in two sorts of space: within us and between us. By 'within us', I mean that each individual makes moral judgements about what we think is right and wrong. This is a matter of conscience. It is the 'between us', however, that is the stuff of politics. This involves shared understandings about what is right, what is wrong and how we adjudicate disputes. Here, the value of what I think is right is measured by the extent to which I can persuade others. The more people I can persuade, the more legitimate my conception of the right. The more legitimate it is, the more likely it is to shape the way that groups, entire nations and their governments, debate, think and – more importantly – act. So, irrespective of the way I apply the just war tradition to the case of Iraq and the judgements I draw from that, it is far from inconsequential that I am in a distinct minority if I think the war to have been justified. More than likely, it is either my reasoning or the weight I give to my moral framework that is defective. The first test, therefore, is a consensus test. To what extent do people agree with my principles, the way I am applying them and the conclusions I reach? If there is a significant gap between what I think and what most other people think, can I account for it in an empirically satisfying fashion without having to revert to the argument that they are applying defective reasoning?

The second parameter is linked to the first and draws on ideas first put forth by the eighteenth-century German philosopher Immanuel Kant. Kant argued that moral principles should be 'universalizable' – that is, they should be applicable to every like circumstance. In other words, if we think we can do something to others in certain circumstances, we must admit that they are entitled to do it to us in similar circumstances. If we cannot tolerate that conclusion we should go back and rethink the principle. To use an example that I will return to in Chapter 5, if we think that it is legitimate to torture people who might give us information likely to save lives, we must admit that our enemies have a right to torture our people if they think that doing so might also save lives. We must, in other words, learn to tolerate torture and rob ourselves of the moral language necessary to condemn torture. To give another example, discussed in greater length in Chapter 4, if we believe that it is legitimate to bomb Afghan civilians because they have implicitly or explicitly supported Al Qaeda and the Taliban, we must admit that Al Qaeda and the Taliban are entitled to bomb American or Australian citizens because of their implied support for a range of other perceived injustices. Of course, this is precisely the argument that Al Qaeda *does* make. If we are in the business of building a moral vocabulary that others can understand, engage with and allow to shape their actions, and that can help us avoid fighting in ways that make it harder to undermine popular support for Al Qaeda, it is vital that both its core principles and the way we apply it are generalizable. Otherwise, our vocabulary will descend into self-serving hypocrisy.

Conclusion

Far from being an oxymoron, ethics are both a pervasive and necessary presence in war. Far from being an unnecessary hindrance in this war on terror, ethical behaviour is a prerequisite for victory. If the key to success lies in undermining popular support for Al Qaeda, and I think that Cronin[36] and Williams are correct to say it is, then we cannot possibly hope to win the war on terror if we behave in ways widely seen as unjust. It is not enough simply to persuade ourselves of the justice of what we do. The crucial thing is that we are *seen* to be behaving justly. Only that way will we build the moral capital necessary to undermine popular support for the terrorists. It is certainly the case that, by historical standards, the number of civilians killed by coalition forces during the initial combat phase in Afghanistan and Iraq was remarkably low. Nevertheless, for those whose relatives, community members and/or co-religionists are on the receiving end, the damage is intolerably high. We must therefore ensure that the damage is legitimate, necessary and limited. This is the moral tightrope that the West is walking in the war on terror.

However, before I get into how well America and its allies are doing with this, it is important to understand the gravity of what is being fought for by considering what's wrong with terrorism.

TWO
What's wrong with terrorism?

The main problem with assessing what is wrong with terrorism is that, while the label is frequently used in public and academic debates to describe a wide variety of violent acts, there is very little agreement about what terrorism actually is. Unless we have a clear understanding of what terrorism is and what sets it apart from other forms of political violence, we cannot know whether terrorism is *always* wrong and whether it is more or less wrong than other types of violence. The first hurdle we need to cross is to understand our purpose in offering a definition – not least because it will be almost impossible to give a definition of terrorism that satisfies every analytic, legal and moral purpose. It is rare for commentators to talk about the purposes of definitions, but it is vitally important because definitions are rarely simple descriptions – and nowhere is this truer than in relation to terrorism.

As pure description, the cliché that one man's terrorist is another man's freedom fighter is wholly accurate. This phrase – often sneered at by the political right as an example of moral relativism – was in fact first coined in relation to Ronald Reagan's position on Nicaragua. The Nicaraguan Health Ministry estimated that by late 1982 the American-backed Contra rebels had killed 3,652 civilians, wounded 4,039 and kidnapped 5,232. The Contras were reportedly 'systematically engaged in the killing of prisoners and the unarmed … and indiscriminate attacks, torture and other outrages against personal dignity'.[1] Were they terrorists? Not according to Reagan. For him, 'these freedom fighters are our brothers, and we owe them our help … They are the moral equivalent of our Founding Fathers and the brave men and women of the French Resistance. We cannot turn away from them.'[2] Others disagreed. Gerald Kaufman, the British Labour Party's Foreign Affairs spokesman at the time, pointed to the Contras' many atrocities against non-combatants when he labelled them terrorists.[3]

Although the cliché does not get us very far towards a moral understanding of terrorism, it is a useful starting point because it reminds us that 'terrorism' is not a descriptive term in the sense commonly meant when we talk about definitions. It is therefore unsurprising that terrorists have not generally labelled themselves as such since the early twentieth century.[4] Nowadays, to call someone a terrorist is as much to criticize them as to describe them. The problem, of course, is that unless we can precisely define it, terrorism will become a morally meaningless term – if this is not already the case.

The tricky thing with moral definitions, however, is that they have to be universalizable and this can prove uncomfortable for both analysts and politicians. If terrorists are defined – as they commonly are – as non-state actors who use violence against governments, then the Warsaw Ghetto uprising was an act of terrorism – indeed, had contemporary British and Australian anti-terrorism legislation prevailed over the Nazi-controlled ghetto, the Jewish rebels would have been guilty of terrorism. If terrorism is defined as a strategy designed to induce fear, as it often is, then the possession of nuclear weapons for deterrence purposes is terrorism. If terrorism is defined – as it will be here – as the deliberate killing of non-combatants, then 9/11 was an act of terrorism, but so too was the destruction of Dresden and Hiroshima.

As difficult as it might be, consistency is vital if we are to put forth and defend a moral definition of terrorism and avoid the perils of relativism. If the term is to have moral relevance we have to accept that our friends and our governments might also, at some time, have been terrorists. This danger has been long recognized by governments which, since the 1937 Convention for the Prevention and Punishment of Terrorism, have been careful not to endorse a legal definition that could indict either political allies or aspects of their own history.[5]

The purpose of this chapter is first to put forth a *moral* definition of terrorism. According to David Rodin, a moral definition attempts to elucidate 'the features of acknowledged core instances of terrorism which merit and explain the moral reaction which most of us have toward them'.[6] This chapter explores what it is about terrorism that makes it *morally* distinguishable from other forms of political violence, as a precursor to an examination of that morality. I will argue that, morally speaking, terrorism is best defined as the deliberate targeting of non-combatants for political purposes.[7] It is this character that marks terrorism out from other types of violence in contemporary public debates. It is also this character that renders terrorism immoral in every circumstance. Seen this way, it is possible to be both a freedom fighter *and* a terrorist. Whether or not one is a freedom fighter is a question relating to the reasons for employing violence and judgements about the moral veracity of those reasons. By this view, whether or not one is a terrorist is entirely dependent on the intended victims of the violence unleashed. If the intended victims are non-combatants, then the perpetrator is a terrorist, irrespective of whether the perpetrator is a government official or rebel, fighting for a good cause or not. The final part of the chapter considers whether terrorism might ever be justifiable and rejects four arguments that hold that it is.

What is terrorism?

The starting point for a moral definition of terrorism should be the everyday usage of the word. Indeed, one of the key reasons why defining terrorism in the abstract has proven so difficult is that its everyday meaning has changed so much in the past century.[8] Early 'terrorists' were often selective about their targets. Members of the nineteenth-century Russian anarchist organization, Narodnaya Volya (1878–81), acted more as assassins, targeting only senior members of Russia's ruling elite or law enforcement agents, sometimes placing themselves in harm's way in order to protect innocent bystanders. In one famous case, in 1878 Vera Zasulich was cleared of attempting to murder the governor-general of St Petersburg despite shooting him at close range and then simply waiting to be apprehended, because the jury concluded that her act was an understandable response to the governor-general's brutal treatment of prisoners. Today, however, there is almost unanimous agreement that the word 'terrorism' has pejorative connotations associated with the bombing, shooting and maiming of non-combatants – but little agreement beyond that. Even the mood of consensus that swept the world after 9/11 did not produce agreement between states about what terrorism was. After one set of protracted negotiations in 2004, Jeremy Greenstock, the British Ambassador to the UN and chair of the UN Security Council's committee on terrorism, conceded that 'it might be easier to define terrorist acts than terrorism generally'.[9] Others put it somewhat differently, suggesting that while terrorism is hard to define precisely, we all know a terrorist act when we see one.

The one thing that is clear about the everyday usage of 'terrorism' is that the term is a pejorative one. It is a label one attaches to particular acts of political violence to delegitimize them. This is a useful starting point for building a moral definition. The second step, then, is to enquire what it is about terrorism that gives it its pejorative connotation. For our purposes, it is worth working through four elements present in most definitions:

1 Terrorism is politically motivated violence.
2 It is conducted by non-state actors.
3 It achieves its aims by creating fear.
4 It intentionally targets non-combatants.

Not all of these are morally reprehensible. Not all acts or campaigns commonly labelled 'terrorist' reflect all these elements, and many violent campaigns not generally considered 'terrorist' do. In order to identify those elements of terrorism that mark it out morally from other types of political violence, we need to ascertain which of these are unjust and why.

Politically motivated violence The idea that terrorism is politically motivated violence distinguishes it from criminal violence and violence caused by mental illness. It may seem surprising nowadays that for many writers in the 1960s and 1970s these two forms of violence were core categories of terrorism.[10] Though less prevalent, these ideas persist today. Is it the case that terrorists are mentally ill? Writing in the immediate aftermath of 9/11, Walter Laqueur – one of the world's best-known terrorism experts – observed that 'madness, especially paranoia, plays a role in contemporary terrorism … The element of madness plays an important role, even if many are reluctant to acknowledge it.'[11] The problem with Laqueur's view is that it is just not true. Psychological studies are almost unanimous in suggesting that most convicted terrorists are not, in fact, mentally ill.[12] Furthermore, neither lone, mentally ill terrorists nor groups that use terrorism for criminal purposes provoke moral dilemmas about the use of violence. They are either simply mentally ill or criminal: they make no claims on our understanding of the morality of violence.[13] Given this, most analyses of terrorism tend to insist that terrorism be understood as political violence.

The idea that terrorism is best understood as political violence is basically sound but it doesn't get us very far towards a moral definition. As I noted in the previous chapter, political violence might be justified in all sorts of circumstances by referring to *jus ad bellum* principles. Identifying terrorism as politically motivated violence does not help us explain why it is condemned or understand its unique character. After all, the just war tradition is concerned with identifying the conditions that may justify political violence. The potentially significant question is therefore not whether terrorism is political but who has the authority to use violence for political purposes?

Non-state actors Many definitions of terrorism include the fact that terrorism is violence unleashed by non-state actors. As I noted earlier, the 1937 Convention on Terrorism defined terrorism as violence against the state.[14] Likewise, some US government agencies continue to regard terrorists as non-state actors and this view is widespread in the literature.[15]

But the idea that only states are entitled to use violence is relatively new. At the beginning of the Middle Ages, two types of actors were identified as legitimate authorities for violence. First, any agent with the power to act publicly could wage justified war. That included kings, princes, barons, dukes, feudal lords and the many other types of noble person who enjoyed authority over others. Gradually the right of private actors to wage war was whittled down until it applied only to sovereigns. The second was the Church, though once again successive restrictions were placed on the Church's participation in war until it evaporated entirely. Today, then, there is a widespread presumption that the sovereign state is the only authority capable of authorizing legitimate political violence, but there is nothing natural or inevitable about that. In fact, using the label 'terrorist' to describe all acts of non-state violence would have us agreeing with the Nazis that the Jews who offered resistance in the Warsaw Ghetto and the French resistance were properly labelled 'terrorists'.

Nowadays, there are at least two possible ways of justifying the use of force by non-state actors. First, many just war theorists and some international lawyers recognize that citizens or subjects have a right to rebel against oppressive governments. Back in the fifth century, St Augustine argued that unjust laws were not true law at all and therefore placed subjects under no obligation. Later proponents of the just war, such as the Oxford-based Renaissance lawyer Gentili and the Spanish scholastic theologian Vitoria, insisted that a government's oppression of its own people could give just cause for war (though for very different reasons). Over time, the liberal idea that sovereignty is bestowed not by God but by the will of the people, conferring on the people a right to use arms in defiance of an oppressive government, became widely accepted. The idea was most clearly set out by one of America's founding fathers, Thomas Jefferson, at the head of the Declaration of Independence. Promulgated on 4 July 1776, the Declaration insisted that:

> We hold these truths to be self-evident, that all men are created equal, that they are endowed by their Creator with certain inalienable Rights, that among these are Life, Liberty and Happiness.

All people have *inalienable* rights, rights that are prior to and privileged over politics and the state. What is more, these rights are so obvious that they are 'self-evident'. They are natural, being endowed by our 'Creator', whatever or whoever we think that is. The Declaration continued:

> To secure these rights, Governments are instituted among Men, deriving their just powers from the consent of the governed – That whenever any Form of Government becomes destructive of these ends, it is the Right of the People to alter or abolish it, and to institute new Government …
>
> … when a long train of abuses and usurpations, pursuing

invariably the same Object evinces a design to reduce them under absolute Despotism, it is their right, it is their duty, to throw off such Government, and to provide new Guards for their future security ...

In other words, according to Jefferson, governments that fail to protect the fundamental rights of their citizens or that wantonly abuse those rights fail in their sovereign responsibilities. This gives the people, as individual sovereigns, the right and duty to overthrow the government and replace it with one more conducive to the satisfaction of their rights.

Of course, these ideas were not widely supported in their own time. American independence was won through force of arms, not the power of persuasion. But although its meaning and fortunes ebbed and flowed, the idea that sovereignty resides with the people has become a cornerstone of modern political life. Thus, a people must logically have the right to use political violence in order to overthrow an oppressive government – as America's founding fathers did.

The second potential avenue for justifying violence by non-state actors is via the widespread recognition that such violence may be justified in cases where the sovereign has either dissolved (as in Somalia and Yugoslavia in the 1990s) or has been unjustly overrun by a foreign power (such as wartime France).

It is not therefore the fact that terrorists can be defined as non-state actors that provides the basis for a moral definition of terrorism, for there are many cases of non-state actors using force quite legitimately. Who now would think of Thomas Jefferson as a terrorist leader? However, it is important that in saying this we do not absolve non-state actors of their responsibility to justify their cause for 'war' in moral terms. In particular, non-state actors who engage in violence must demonstrate that they are a 'legitimate authority' that acts in accordance with the will of the people.

Spreading fear Another element common to many definitions of terrorism is the idea that terrorism seeks to accomplish its goals by spreading fear. The aim is to create a general climate of fear within society that will coerce those in authority to accede to the terrorists' demands. It is the spread of fear, Elshtain argues, that makes terrorism particularly dangerous because 'none of the goods human beings cherish – including politics itself – can flourish absent a measure of civic peace and security'.[16]

Viewing terrorism as a strategy of instilling fear (through violence) for political purposes has a number of definitional advantages. Most significantly, as Robert Goodin points out in his book-length defence of this definition, it places the 'terror' back in 'terrorism'.[17] The word 'terror' is associated with supreme fear, so terrorism must logically mean a strategy of violence designed to create fear and thereby change the political behaviour of the intended target. More often than not, terrorism textbooks argue that terrorists kill non-combatants in order either to scare them into pressuring their government to change its policies or to provoke an over-reaction from the government that will undermine the relative legitimacy of its cause. The use of fear or terror as a method of war is particularly wrong because it breaches the Kantian injunction that humans should not be used as means and threatens the welfare of civil society as a whole.

Understanding terrorism in this way makes supreme etymological sense. After all, were not the first modern terrorists the self-proclaimed *terreurs* of the French Revolution who used fear of the guillotine to maintain order? Actually, the French Revolutionary picture was much more complex. The labelling of revolutionary justice as 'The Terror' was invented by the Revolution's enemies – principally the Jacobins who overthrew Robespierre and the conservative British writer and politician Edmund Burke. On closer inspection we find that, however deadly, the Terror was formally legislated as a means of punishing those guilty of plotting against the state, not of creating fear. In the face of foreign invasion and mob violence, Danton called for 'judicial measures to punish counter-revolutionaries', proposing 'a new-fledged tribunal speaking the law'.[18] With important exceptions such as the political executions of the Hébertists and Dantonists at the Terror's climax, the majority of victims were targeted on an individual basis for specific wrongs they were meant to have inflicted upon the Republic. Indeed, there is a broad consensus that, between 1792 and 1794, approximately ninety per cent of all the Terror's victims were judicially sanctioned executions involving individuals accused of insurrection, collusion or plotting against the Republic.[19] Not all of those who were denounced were imprisoned, and only around half of those accused of crimes warranting execution were in fact executed.[20] Crucially, the use of violence to instil fear played very little part in the Jacobins' strategy. For them, the executions represented the exercise of the law – however misguided – against those guilty of treason against the state.

Once we discard the putative etymological roots of 'terrorism', the idea that the distinctiveness of terrorism comes from its intention to instil fear starts to look less persuasive, especially if we remember that terrorism is generally considered to be a particularly repugnant form of political violence. Indeed, it would be perverse to suggest that pursuing policy change through the threat of violence was less justifiable than actually using violence. Historically, states have often used 'coercive diplomacy' – the threat of force to persuade others to change their course of action – as a way of resolving disputes without the need for war. Moreover, the social consequences of terrorism that Elshtain mentions may also be the foreseeable consequences of justifiable wars. Finally, it is not at all clear that terrorists *do* in fact pick their targets in such a way as to create generalized fear. Some terrorists – especially the Russian anarchists of the nineteenth century – assassinated specific individuals; others attack general types of target such as government buildings or transport nodes; while others, such as Al Qaeda, seek the physical destruction of their enemies. To put it bluntly, Osama bin Laden wants to kill us, not scare us.

Targets non-combatants It is the fourth element of most definitions of terrorism that renders it so immoral: the direct and intentional targeting of non-combatants. As I argued in the previous chapter, the principle of discrimination is one of the most steadfast of all the just war principles and is expressed clearly in contemporary international law. The principle holds that non-combatants should be immune from direct attack.

The first attempts to define groups of people who were to be immune during war came in the thirteenth century under Pope Gregory IX. Then, people were granted immunity either if the social function they fulfilled was essential for the life of the community or if they held divine office.[21] Vitoria expanded the immunity to all 'innocent' people, by which he implicitly meant non-combatants. Any act of war that deliberately killed non-combatants or that used non-combatants as a means to an end was unjust, Vitoria argued. There are a number of compelling moral, prudential and legal arguments to support the principle of non-combatant immunity, which help to explain why this is one of the most clearly expressed international legal rules. Although groups frequently do deliberately kill non-combatants, there is almost universal global agreement that they should not. The ethics and laws of war impose a complete ban on the direct intentional targeting of non-combatants. Moreover, under the Rome Statute of the International Criminal Court, the leaders of more than a hundred states would face criminal charges if they ordered such acts. It is worth noting, briefly, Colm McKeogh's seven reasons for supporting the principle of non-combatant immunity:

1 Non-combatants have committed no wrong and therefore they may not have war waged upon them.
2 Non-combatants are not participating in the fighting.
3 Non-combatants are unable to defend themselves.
4 Killing non-combatants is militarily unnecessary.
5 Maintaining non-combatant immunity reduces the casualties of war.
6 Sparing women, children and those who perform essential peacetime functions is essential for species survival.
7 Killing non-combatants is contrary to the laws of war.[22]

So, by this account, modern society believes terrorism to be wrong because it entails killing those who ought not to be killed. As Douglas Lackey put it:

> What separates the terrorist from the traditional revolutionary is a persistent refusal to direct violence at military objectives. Terrorism, on this account, is the threat or use of force against non-combatants for political purposes. In ordinary war, the deaths

of civilians are side effects of military operations directed against military targets. In terrorist operations, the civilian is the direct and intentional target of attack.[23]

A moral definition of terrorism

The only element of terrorism that marks it out as particularly immoral is its intentional targeting of non-combatants. Hence, I offer a moral definition of terrorism as being the deliberate targeting of non-combatants for political purposes. Not surprisingly, this definition has been widely criticized, and before I move on to consider arguments that seek to justify the deliberate killing of non-combatants in certain circumstances, it is important to examine the objections to the definition offered.

Firstly, Gerry Wallace rejects the 'absolutist' view that it is always wrong to kill non-combatants, arguing that 'in certain circumstances there are equally powerful and accessible intuitions which support the opposite view'.[24] In circumstances where killing the innocent is the only way to prosecute a justifiable war, Wallace argues that the distinction between combatants and non-combatants can be put aside.[25] This leads Khatchadourian to suggest that the prohibition on killing innocent people can be 'set aside' (Wallace's term) or 'restricted' (Khatchadourian's) if the terrorist's community is under attack and killing the innocent is the only means of self-defence.[26] Wallace and Khatchadourian thus argue that the principle of non-combatant immunity itself should be restricted on consequentialist grounds. The question here ultimately boils down to whether one accepts the view that there are, or should be, restrictions on the scope of non-combatant immunity. I will return to this question in more detail later, but certainly the just war tradition and internationally agreed rules about the conduct of war steadfastly rejected this position and neither Wallace nor Khatchadourian give us good reason to doubt the validity of this view.

Another type of argument is that the moral definition of terrorism is counter-intuitive. That is, the definition forces us to label as 'terrorist' some acts that we would not normally choose to label so, and to label others that most agree *are* terrorism something else. As an example of the former, Robert Young points to the 1978 kidnapping of former Italian Prime Minister Aldo Moro by the Red Brigade and the 1984 Brighton bombing where the IRA attempted to blow up Margaret Thatcher and members of the British Cabinet. He claims that in neither case could the intended target be usefully defined as 'innocent', yet both attacks were labelled terrorist. According to Young, classifying these attacks as something other than terrorism 'may save the moralized definition but are unhelpful to the careful analysis of the phenomenon of terrorism'.[27]

Common to many moral accounts of terrorism, however, Young's argument confuses the distinction between innocence and guilt with the distinction between combatants and non-combatants. Unless one believes that private individuals and groups have a right summarily to determine an individual's guilt or innocence and execute them without due process – a belief that, thankfully, is not shared very widely – the relative moral guilt or innocence of an individual is irrelevant to the question of whether they can be justly attacked. It is only individuals' status as combatants that permits their attack. It is for courts, not self-appointed vigilantes, to decide an individual's guilt or innocence. In the two cases cited, if the intended victims were properly described as combatants (a view I do not share, because the UK was not at war with the IRA and neither was Italy at war with the Red Brigades; moreover, the IRA and Red Brigades would have to satisfy the *jus ad bellum* criteria legitimately to impose combatant status on their enemies, and neither of them did), there would be no good grounds for inciting public moral outrage by labelling acts that targeted them as 'terrorism'. If the attackers failed to satisfy the *jus ad bellum* criteria, as I think they did, then both acts were simply cases of unlawful and immoral violence. If they did satisfy the criteria, both must be interpreted as legitimate acts of war.

My own view is that both examples are indeed cases of terrorism, precisely because the intended victims were non-combatants. In the Italian case, a former prime minister was clearly a non-combatant because any potential combatancy was tied to the office he formerly held. In no way, shape or form was Moro making a military contribution to a war. The Brighton case is a little more complex, but because the IRA failed to satisfy the *jus ad bellum* criteria and because – whatever the IRA might have argued – the British government was not at war, Thatcher and her Cabinet were non-combatants.

An example of a case where my definition would lead us to label acts commonly thought of as terrorism as something else is provided by Virginia Held, who points to the 1983 attack on the US Marine barracks in Lebanon perpetrated by Hezbollah, which killed 241 people, mostly Marines. According to the moral definition offered here, this attack would not be considered 'terrorist' because the targets were military personnel. According to Held, such a judgement 'seems arbitrary'.[28] But to argue that this was not an act of terrorism is not to argue that it was justified. On closer inspection, the crucial moral judgement in this case and the source of our condemnation is rooted in *jus ad bellum*, not *jus in bello*. This can be seen by transplanting the act itself (driving a truckload of explosives into a military barracks) into a different context. Would we condemn a French resistance fighter as a terrorist if she drove a truckload of explosives into a German military barracks in 1942 France? No. We would argue that this was a legitimate and properly directed act of war against an unjust invader. So, we condemn the attack in Lebanon not because of the nature of the attack itself (*jus in bello*), but because it targeted soldiers who we believed were justly stationed in Lebanon and because we do not believe that Hezbollah had a legitimate *jus ad bellum* licence to wage war on America.

If it is to make moral sense, 'terrorism' must refer to an act, not to particular groups that happen to oppose the powerful. The danger of labelling everything as 'terrorism' is moral inconsistency, which ultimately breeds moral relativism. My point is that we have other words to describe types of violence that do not satisfy the conditions of the moral definition offered here. As soon as we broaden the definition of terrorism we lose consistency; any serious moral discussion of terrorism has to apply the label consistently, even if doing so produces results that we find uncomfortable.

The third type of criticism holds that it is not as easy to draw a distinction between combatant and non-combatant as the moral definition offered here suggests.[29] This is a criticism often levelled at the just war tradition as a whole. Admittedly, there are plenty of grey areas. Are civilians who work in dual-use plants (such as an engine factory that makes engines for cars and tanks) legitimate targets? Are all members of an oppressive regime or occupying power combatants, or only those directly involved in fighting? Are police officers combatants? Are off-duty soldiers and police officers? These are grey area questions that can be evaluated only on a case-by-case basis, because moral judgements will ultimately relate to the context and the contribution that particular groups are making to a country's war-fighting effort. But these cases do not undermine the basic idea or moral value of the distinction between combatants and non-combatants. On the one hand, they are a minority of cases. On the other hand, the very fact that they are considered a grey area and in need of special deliberation with due attention to the context is a product of the combatant/non-combatant distinction. Removing or downplaying the distinction would lessen the moral significance of these questions, reduce the need for fine-grained moral judgements and – ultimately – make non-combatants more vulnerable. Eroding the centrality of the combatant/non-combatant distinction plays into the hands of one of the central justifications of terrorism: that there are no non-combatants.

Thus, there are no good grounds for doubting that terrorism involves the deliberate targeting of non-combatants for political purposes. It follows from this that terrorism is always wrong. Unsurprisingly, however, things do not end here because defenders of terrorism have offered a number of ways of justifying the deliberate targeting of non-combatants for political purposes.

Justifications of terrorism

This section examines four types of justification for terrorism. To provide a plausible exception to the prohibition on killing, each justification would need to present a wholly convincing case, predicated on some moral principle thought more important than that of non-combatant immunity. None of them accomplishes this task.

Consequentialism Consequentialists insist that we should judge an act by its outcomes. Violent means employed to achieve worthwhile ends are considered legitimate, even if the means are morally or legally proscribed, if they accomplish their – presumably justifiable – aim.[30] This view clearly contradicts the principle of non-combatant immunity by making non-combatants a means to an ends. There are two types of consequentialist justification of terrorism: utilitarianism and what may be described as the 'anti-oppression exception'.[31]

The utilitarian argument holds that terrorism may be preferable to conventional war because it is a less costly way of fighting. The US used this lesser-evil argument to justify the atomic terror attacks on Hiroshima and Nagasaki. Although horrific, the argument goes, far fewer people died as a result of the atomic attacks than would have died as a result of a conventional invasion of Japan. This position reflects the view of the famous American Civil War General, William T. Sherman, that because the evils of war cannot be lessened, the most moral thing to do is to bring war to as speedy and inexpensive an end as possible through the use of overwhelming violence and terror if necessary.

There are a number of problems with this position. It is always an uncertain calculus. In the case of Japan, historians are bitterly divided on whether the atomic attacks reduced the overall amount of bloodshed. Many argue that Japan was already prepared to surrender or that given Japan's weakened state, Truman's estimation of the costs of invasion was grossly overestimated. This account also fails to justify why non-combatants should forgo their rights in order to protect the lives of combatants.[32] The utilitarian argument requires us to accept the murder of non-combatants in order (possibly) to save some other combatants and non-combatants. Ultimately, it requires us to believe that non-combatants have no special rights at all, a position at odds with centuries of moral and legal thinking about war. Of course, the principle works both ways and the real test comes in whether we would be prepared to confer the same rights on our enemies. If the utilitarians are right, then the German bombing of London and Coventry and its extermination of Russian POWs were justifiable if the Nazis genuinely believed that these actions would shorten the war. This is an intolerable position that exposes the moral vacuity of the utilitarian position.

The second type of consequentialism – the 'anti-oppression exception' – holds that terrorism is justified when it is a weapon of the weak wielded against oppressors. It is widely acknowledged that if we obliged the weak to follow the same rules as the strong, they would never prevail, even when they had justice on their side. According to Kai Nielsen, 'revolutionary terrorism' is justifiable when the terrorists have good reason to believe that their violent acts might be effective and so long as the suffering caused by terrorism is lower overall than the suffering inflected by the current order.[33] Aside from terrorists themselves, one of the most prominent advocates of this position was the French writer Jean-Paul Sartre. With the Algerian struggle for independence from France in mind, Sartre argued that advocating non-violence to the subjects of oppression constituted a form of complicity in oppression.[34] Instead, he supported the idea of terrorist violence on behalf of the oppressed as the only realistic way of ending their oppression.[35]

This particular argument has long been popular among apologists for terrorism. In an 1849 essay on 'Murder', Karl Heinzen – a radical publicist with anarchist leanings – argued that the voluntary killing of another human was a 'crime against humanity'. 'No one under any pretext', he wrote, 'has the right to destroy another's life and … anyone who does kill another … is quite simply a murderer.'[36] He continued, 'if to kill is always a crime, then it is forbidden equally to all; if it is not a crime, then it is permitted equally to all'. Given that oppressors kill to maintain their privileged position, murder 'is still a necessity, an unavoidable instrument in the achievement of historical ends' for if oppressors 'can justify murder, even going so far as to claim a special privilege in the matter, then necessity compels us to challenge this privilege'. In other words, the weak are entitled to use murder to defeat oppression because the oppressors use murder and other forms of structural violence to maintain their rule. In these terms, terrorists understand themselves as acting in self-defence.

There are three problems with this position. First, if a terrorist can justly ignore non-combatants' rights, it follows that the victims of terrorist attacks can also ignore the rights of those whom the terrorists claim to represent. This renders the terrorists' initial justification nonsensical because the right can no longer be said to exist. Second, providing an 'anti-oppression' exception to non-combatant immunity creates the potential for abuse, ultimately undermining the values that terrorists claim to be defending. Third, the idea that terrorism is a form of 'self-defence' overlooks the nature of terrorist violence itself. On closer inspection it seems clear that targeting non-combatants does nothing directly to protect the would-be terrorist or his/her 'constituents' from imminent or actual attack.

Collective responsibility An alternative justification of terrorism rejects the distinction between combatant and non-combatant altogether. Many terrorist organizations, apologists and a handful of scholars argue that non-combatants who benefit materially from an oppressive regime lose their 'innocence' and become legitimate targets. This position holds that non-combatants who benefit from an oppressive regime or who fail to oppose it are as guilty as the oppressors themselves.

Referring to the terror bombing of Nazi Germany, Burleigh Wilkins argues that only those Germans who actively resisted the Nazis and renounced all the benefits that accrued from membership of the Nazi state should have been immune from attack.[37] According to Wilkins, in such circumstances it is legitimate to target non-combatants provided two conditions are met. First, that all political and legal avenues be exhausted before force is countenanced, and second, that 'terrorism will be directed against members of a community or group which is collectively guilty of violence'.[38] Wilkins admits that this means legitimizing violence 'upon those who in their individual capacity may have done or intended no harm to the would-be terrorists or to the community or group to which they belong'.[39]

Similarly, the French intellectual Frantz Fanon defended terrorism in the name of anti-colonialism on the grounds that non-combatant colonizers profited handsomely from colonial oppression.[40] Terrorist organizations themselves frequently refer to the collective responsibility argument to justify targeting non-combatants. For instance, Al Qaeda evoked Wilkins's argument when it held Americans – 'civilians and military' – collectively responsible for the US military presence in the Middle East and its support for Israel.[41]

There are many problems with the doctrine of collective responsibility. Most troublingly, it equates non-combatancy with 'innocence' and combatancy with 'guilt' and sets up the terrorist as a self-appointed judge, jury and executioner. Some of the earliest just war theorists and canon lawyers did the same thing until it became clear that this reasoning provided a rationale for mass slaughter. If communities could be held collectively responsible for crimes, why not slaughter all those who survive – men, women, children – after a battle is won? Over time, the just war tradition developed the distinction between combatants and non-combatants as a way of limiting the violence of war by insisting that it is only an actor's actions – their practical contribution to a belligerent's war-fighting effort – that renders them liable for attack. The idea of collective responsibility removes this limit in the most dramatic way.

Second, as with consequentialism, collective responsibility erodes the very rights that terrorists claim for themselves. A justifiable violent struggle against oppression is a struggle for the preservation of human rights, the most basic of these being the right to life. There are only two circumstances in which an individual loses that right – both by his or her own volition. The first is by joining the armed forces. As Walzer argues, the soldier loses his or her right not to be targeted by the enemy in return for a right to kill enemy soldiers without moral blame. The second is by being found guilty by an authoritative and legitimate court of a crime punishable by death. The doctrine of collective responsibility removes this fundamental right to life and makes it conditional on an individual's relationship to perceived oppression. The right to life thus made conditional, the terrorist organization loses one of its central means of justification.

Third, there is an empirical problem. Wilkins, Fanon and others all argue that terrorism against oppression produces a more just social order by removing and punishing those guilty of oppression. Unfortunately, they provide no evidence to support this claim.[42] Fourth, there is a question of moral consistency. If communities can be collectively judged for their wrongdoing, why cannot the victims of terrorism hold the terrorists and their constituent communities collectively responsible and punish them for their terrorism in kind? The 'anti-oppression exception' is based on a naïve belief that it is easy to determine justice and injustice in an objective fashion. That being so, terrorists can appoint themselves as moral judges and executioners. Whole groups can then be attacked simply on the basis of a judgement by the terrorists and their philosopher-allies in the academy. In reality, conceptions of justice are subjective and in most (but not all) cases both sides to a conflict may have a reasonably justifiable cause. Moreover, even in clear-cut armed struggles, an individual's guilt or innocence may be quite difficult to determine. Finally, this account has a strong affinity with the totalitarianism of Hitler and Stalin as it slates people for death on the basis on their thoughts, opinions and relative economic standing.

Supreme emergency According to the influential ethicist, Michael Walzer, there are situations where the danger confronted is so great and the options so limited that it requires the use of measures expressly barred by the ethics and laws of war.[43] He labels these situations 'supreme emergencies'. Emergencies become supreme when two conditions are satisfied. First, the danger must be imminent. It must be so imminent that states and societies are left with no alternative but to waive the rights of enemy non-combatants.[44] The second element is the nature of the threat being confronted. The threat, Walzer tells us, 'must be of an unusual and horrifying kind', in other words, it must shock the conscience of humanity.[45] Political communities face a supreme emergency only when the costs of losing are catastrophic, when defeat will lead to annihilation and massacre.

Walzer uses the British decision to bombard German cities in 1941 to illustrate his argument. According to Walzer, although Britain was justified in overriding the principle of non-combatant immunity, its decision to do so was a moral tragedy and the political leadership was quite correct to refuse to honour Arthur Harris, the head of Bomber Command, at the end of the war. Nevertheless, the decision was legitimate because 'utilitarian calculation can force us to violate the rules of war only when we are face-to-face not merely with defeat but with defeat likely to bring disaster to the political community'.[46] In such cases, Walzer suggests, leaders lose their agency: they are simply compelled to do whatever they can to defend their political community. A leader who refuses to take this decision errs by placing his or her own moral values above the well-being of the political community he or she has been charged with protecting.

It is not difficult to see how the supreme emergency argument can be applied to terrorism – though it is important to note that Walzer himself does not think that it does. It implies an important but subtle modification of the 'anti-oppression exception' described earlier. In the case of a supreme emergency, the rule of non-combatant immunity remains intact but is temporarily overridden to accomplish the lesser evil. This position was expressed by Sheikh Fadlallah, one of Hezbollah's spiritual guides, in the 1980s. Fadlallah, like many Palestinians, sincerely believed that the Palestinians confronted a 'supreme emergency'. Forced by the million to leave their lands and live in refugee camps, Palestinians, he believed, were the victims of slow-motion genocide. Fadlallah justified the use of 'unconventional' means by reference to the Palestinians' right to self-defence and the imbalance of power. This alone, however, was not enough to justify the direct targeting of non-combatants. Fadlallah insisted that such attacks were justifiable only 'on an enemy whom it is impossible to fight by conventional means'.[47] Thus, he argued, Palestinians faced a threat to their very survival and had no reasonable alternative ways of defending themselves. In other words, they faced a supreme emergency.

Unsurprisingly, the supreme emergency argument encounters many of the same problems as consequentialism and collective responsibility. I have argued elsewhere that it contradicts the rest of Walzer's rights-based just war theory; it undermines the principle of non-combatant immunity and opens the door to abuse; it is predicated on the fallacious assumption that there are sometimes no alternatives to killing non-combatants; and it draws on a misplaced strategic belief that targeting non-combatants can defend a group facing a supreme emergency.[48] On top of that, Walzer himself has since argued vigorously against terrorism, insisting that it cannot be justified in supreme emergency terms unless 'the oppression to which the terrorists claimed to be responding was genocidal in character'. There are few such cases, Walzer argued, because terrorism is used more as a tool for securing political success than for avoiding disastrous defeat.[49] Indeed, Walzer would reject Fadlallah's claim of slow-motion genocide in Palestine, insisting that genocide consist of an observable pattern of massacre to trigger the supreme emergency exception.

Divine mandate A further type of justification for terrorism is the claim that some killing is commanded by God. Much like the Christian crusaders in the eleventh century, religiously oriented terrorists often claim that they have been authorized by God to launch terrorist attacks.[50] Yitzhak Rabin's assassin claimed a divine mandate, as have many Christian anti-abortion terrorists in the US.[51] Of course, the most (in)famous proponent of the divine mandate is Osama bin Laden. Bin Laden told an ABC reporter that 'Allah is the one who created us and blessed us with this religion, and orders [us] to carry out our holy struggle – jihad – to raise the word of Allah above all the words of unbelievers'.[52] One of the main problems with the divine mandate argument is that it is impossible to disprove, it can be claimed by almost anyone, and it can be used to justify anything. There is no limit whatsoever on what God can reputedly 'command'.

The question of divine mandate created problems for medieval and early Renaissance just war thinkers precisely because it could be invoked to justify anything – particularly in an age when kings and popes claimed to be directly appointed by God. In the sixteenth century, Vitoria argued against the divine mandate on the grounds that there was no precedent and no direct proof that God had in fact commanded particular wars. Vitoria left open the possibility that God could theoretically issue a mandate for war but insisted that those claiming such a mandate provide evidence of its existence. We could say much the same today in response to terrorists who claim a divine mandate. Religious believers must accept the theoretical possibility that God could issue a mandate for war, but those invoking such a mandate are required to prove its existence by more than just faith. Given that today, as in Vitoria's time, there remains no precedent for such a mandate, it must be admitted that the likelihood of a terrorist group furnishing compelling evidence to support its claim to a divine mandate is, at best, very slim.

Conclusion

Terrorism involves the deliberate killing of non-combatants and is always wrong because of that fact. This brings us to the question of whether acts of terrorism provide sufficient grounds for war, as advocates of the global war on terror have maintained. This is the question for the following chapter.

THREE
A just war on terror?

Immediately after the terrorist attacks of 11 September 2001, President George W. Bush called for a 'war against terrorism'.[1] Terrorists, the President argued, do not merely kill people, they also threaten the democratic way of life.[2] Thus, 'our war on terror begins with Al Qaeda, but it does not end there. It will not end until every terrorist group of global reach has been found, stopped and defeated.'[3] Since then, the US has used force to overthrow the regimes in Afghanistan and Iraq and has reoriented its national security strategy to create a right of pre-emptive self-defence for itself. Commentators have had much to say about whether elements of the war on terror are strategically and politically prudent or legal. They have focused much less, however, on the question of whether the war as a whole war is just. Although questions of prudence and legality are important ones, it is also important to ask whether what is being done in our name is 'right'. As Oliver O'Donovan pointed out, 'these decisions are, on the one hand, *ours*, and not to be thrown off on to others' shoulders with a shudder of irritated editorialising'.[4]

We need to begin by noting that war is not an *inevitable* response to terrorism. Indeed, a much more common, less costly and often more successful approach is to tackle it by using criminal justice. Although the US resorted to war, the UK responded to the 7/7 attacks on London in the same way that Spain responded to the Madrid bombings – by seeing terrorism as a criminal offence and using the criminal justice system to punish the perpetrators. Approaching terrorism in this way has several important advantages over waging war. Not only is it more effective in bringing terrorists to justice, it is also much more legitimate, precise and cost-effective. I noted in Chapter 1 than an effective 'war on terror' has to be a legitimate one, lest it inadvertently create more terrorists. The best way of ensuring this is to see terrorism, not as an act of war, but as a criminal justice problem. Doing so would rob political leaders of the popular lexicon of war but it would make for a more effective long-term counter-terrorism strategy. After all, non-state terrorists of the Al Qaeda type have never actually toppled democratic governments and nor is there much likelihood of them doing so. As such, it would seem to make little sense to tackle terrorism through the prism of war. In addition, as the nineteenth-century Prussian strategist Carl von Clausewitz[5] teaches us, war is an unpredictable and uncontrollable phenomenon. Once unleashed, it is difficult to control its course and impossible to account for its unforeseen and unintended consequences. War takes on its own logic of escalation that makes it a particularly unsuitable means for achieving precise ends.

There is a further reason why seeing terrorism as a criminal justice problem is preferable to viewing it as a war. 'War', commonly understood, is a violent confrontation between two entities that enjoy certain rights. Combatants in wars are protected by the laws of war and acquire a certain degree of legitimacy. No matter how hard governments try to prevent it by, for example, inventing new legal categories such as 'illegal combatants', waging war on terrorists confers a degree of legitimacy upon them. It would be much better, therefore, for liberal democratic governments to pursue terrorists through the criminal justice system than through war.

The second key point to make at the outset is that just because terrorism is a grave wrong and the commission of terrorist acts may create a just cause for war, it does not necessarily follow that a 'war on terror' is just. Vitoria argued in the sixteenth century that not every wrong endured constitutes a good reason for waging war. Some wrongs are simply not 'wrong enough' to warrant recourse to force; others might warrant only limited recourse to force. It is therefore important to resist the temptation, so evident in the West after 9/11, simply to assume that those opposing terrorism have just grounds for war that require no further scrutiny. In addition – a point I will return to later – it is also important not to accept the view that a single justification for war under the rubric of the war on terror suffices to justify a wide range of only tangentially connected military actions, including invasions of Afghanistan and Iraq and bombing raids on Somalia and Yemen.

I begin this chapter by asking whether it is legitimate to wage a war on terror itself. Finding that it is logically impossible to fight a morally justified 'war on terror' – principally because there is no agreement about who the targets are and because, as I argued in the previous chapter, terrorism is a tactic not an actor – I move on to explore whether some of the manifestations of the war on terror have been justifiable, though without getting too much into the question of pre-emptive self-defence, which is the topic of the following chapter. The overall purpose of this chapter is to argue that while some aspects of the war on terror are undoubtedly just, we need to interrogate each *jus ad bellum* case put forward for the use of force individually. Morally speaking, there is no such thing as a 'just war against terrorism' because one can only legitimately wage war against specific combatants representing identifiable groups or entities.

The jus ad bellum test

The war on terror has involved efforts to challenge some of the basic rules governing the use of force, including those stating when it is permissible to launch a war of self-defence and those regulating the treatment of prisoners – the subject matter for the next two chapters. These instances of rule breaking or rule changing – depending on your perspective – since September 11 have been justified in terms of the necessity of defeating an immediate threat to American security. This basically realist argument holds that rigidly adhering to *jus ad bellum* and *jus in bello* criteria would impede the effectiveness of the anti-terrorism campaign.

In addition to the arguments in favour of ethical scrutiny charted in Chapter 1, there are at least three good reasons for using the just war tradition to interrogate the legitimacy of waging a war against terror in the first place. First of all, academics, politicians and public commentators in the West have appropriated the language and concepts of the just war tradition to shape political debate. Although they have sought to avoid ethical scrutiny by declaring unlimited war and denouncing political opponents as 'terrorist sympathizers', political leaders in the US, UK, Australia and other states have repeatedly invoked the language of just war to support their claims for waging war in Afghanistan, Iraq and elsewhere. Indeed, some of the most vocal supporters of the war on terror and wars in Afghanistan and Iraq have been leading American just war theorists such as Jean Bethke Elshtain and James Turner Johnson. Although much more muted, opponents of the military response to September 11 have also referred to just war thinking to make the contrary argument.

Second, even when not consciously referred to, the just war tradition is deeply embedded in the way that Westerners think about the legitimacy of going to war. Ideas about just cause, legitimate authority and proportionality have for some time shaped the way Western societies wage war. Of course, saying that the just war tradition is 'embedded' in the way that Western states, societies and militaries think about war is not to say that they always conduct themselves in a just fashion. As I noted in Chapter 1, even at the peak of their influence, classical just war theorists could not determine the actual course of war. What they could do, and what the tradition still does today, is provide a common language with which to evaluate the competing moral claims of war.

The third reason for using the just war tradition to evaluate the legitimacy of the war against terrorism is that this moral tradition approximates closely to agreed international standards of behaviour in relation to recourse to force. Although the tradition has a Western and Christian heritage, it now stretches beyond the borders of Christendom. Most of the world's state and social leaders accept, in some form, the basic principles of the just war tradition as it relates to the decision to wage war.[6] As James Turner Johnson once argued, the international law on armed conflict and international humanitarian law are both 'deeply consistent with the moral requirements of just war'.[7] For these reasons, the just war tradition is the closest thing we have to a 'common morality' when it comes to judgements about the use of force.

How, then, are we to make use of the just war tradition to evaluate the justness of the war against terror? We should avoid the temptation of thinking of just war principles as a coherent set of ideas that we can simply use as a checklist to evaluate particular instances of violence, as is so often the case with moral analyses of war. The principles have evolved and changed over the past few hundred years and we should be careful to ensure that we place them in their proper historical context. What that means for us in the contemporary world is that we should take seriously the rules set down by international law because they reflect a broad degree of consensus about the ethics of war that translates general principles into concrete prescriptions, though the law does not cover the full spectrum of moral reasoning about the decision to wage war. As a result, we should not ask whether just war considerations 'override' legal norms when the two sets of ideas seem to collide, nor vice versa, but instead we should seek an appropriate balance between these different sets of claims – a theme I will reiterate in some of the subsequent chapters.

I will briefly set out what international law has to say about recourse to force. The basic rule, included in Article 2 (4) of the UN Charter, is that states must not use either force or the threat of force in their dealings with each other. In other words, the laws governing the decision to use force rest on a blanket ban. There are only two exceptions. First of all, Article 51 recognizes each state's 'inherent right' to use force in self-defence, 'in the event of an armed attack'. The question of whether this entitles states to use force pre-emptively – that is prior to an imminently expected attack – is hotly debated and is the subject of the following chapter. The second exception – often overlooked by just war theorists who are quick to denounce the legal order for its 'presumption against aggressive war' which, they argue, undermines the place of justice by focusing exclusively on who use force first – is that the Security Council is entitled to authorize collective military enforcement measures whenever it identifies a threat to international peace and security. To do this, the Council needs a majority of nine votes (from a membership of fifteen). The five permanent members of the Security Council (US, UK, Russia, China, France) each hold a veto. Although much maligned and certainly responsible for the Council's failure to act in many urgent cases, the veto is important for ensuring that the UN avoids a situation where it authorizes war against a great power or where it so alienates a great power that it simply walks away from the UN – a fate that befell the League of Nations, which preceded the UN. Outside self-defence and Security Council authorization there are no legal grounds for waging war.

A just cause?

The first, and most pressing, problem is the question of whom are we waging war on and why? Without a clear answer it would be very difficult – if not impossible – to satisfy the *jus ad bellum* requirements of just cause, right intention and proportionality and the international legal requirements set out in the preceding chapter. The most obvious just cause relates to self-defence – the subject of the following chapter. However, it is important to start by noting that the US government did not define the war on terror in narrowly defensive terms. The Bush administration, as we saw at the beginning of this chapter, insisted that the war on terror was being waged against groups worldwide who used terrorist violence to undermine the democratic way of life. Given that I have defined terrorism as any act of violence that seeks deliberately to kill non-combatants for political purposes, this casts the net very widely indeed.

Taking Bush at his word on what the war on terror is about raises an interesting problem. Viewed this way, the war on terror is neither primarily about 9/11 nor is it a war of self-defence. It involves actively seeking out governments and groups that use terrorist violence to undermine and threaten democracy. Thus, although individual military actions commonly seen as part of the war on terror might be best thought of and justified in terms of self-defence – and here, the war in Afghanistan is the clearest example – it is important to recognize that the Bush administration did not conceive the war on terror as such as a war of self-defence. If we understand the war on terror – as Bush clearly wanted us to – as a war on an ideology of terrorism designed to destroy democracy, the war becomes a form of humanitarian crusade – its aim being to prevent deliberate acts of violence against non-combatants and punish the perpetrators. This is a vision that sits comfortably with the neoconservatives, who have long called for America to use its preponderant military power to advance the cause of democracy and liberalism worldwide. This in itself is a seemingly noble aim that enjoys some strong support from the just war tradition. But there are good grounds for doubting the veracity of Bush's claims – not least because the war on terror has been characterized by the large-scale and systematic abuse of human rights, the denigration of democratic liberties at home and international alliances with some of the world's worst human rights abuses. Nevertheless, it is worth exploring the reliability of this line of thinking in a little more detail.

The evolution of just war thinking about the use of force to protect people from grave wrongs such as terrorism can be divided into three broad epochs. In the first two epochs (fourth century–1945), there was a broad consensus (though not unanimity) that severe violations of natural law, such as the deliberate killing of the innocent, could be legitimately halted and punished by any appropriate actors, using war if necessary. Indeed, some writers insisted that there was a moral duty to do so, though this argument became quite rare after the Middle Ages. In the third epoch (post-1945) a consensus developed around the legal prohibitions described earlier, causing a radical separation between law and ethics that has encouraged some contemporary ethicists to argue that ethical concerns should simply override legal rules when the two collide.

In the first epoch, which extends from Augustine in the fourth century to the early Middle Ages, Christendom was formally (if not physically) united in a common political and ethical space. During this period, there was a broad consensus that political leaders had an almost universal *duty* to uphold justice. Early just war writers insisted that the principal just cause for war was to 'right a wrong' and punish evil. As St Thomas Aquinas put it:

> A just cause is required, namely that those who are attacked should be attacked because they deserve it on account of some fault ... true religion does not look upon as sinful those wars that are waged not for motives of aggrandisement, or cruelty, but with the object of securing peace, of punishing evildoers and uplifting the good.[8]

Secular rulers had a responsibility to uphold the law throughout Christendom and a divine duty to protect the innocent from harm. Sovereignty provided no bar to action nor did it limit the geographical extent of a ruler's obligations. There were three reasons for this.

First, the extent of a ruler's domain was not geographically settled, as it is today. Second, the divinely constituted natural law appealed to by Aquinas was binding on all Christians. Third, sovereignty provided no barrier, in part because political entities were not wholly sovereign and because unjust laws were not to be considered law at all. However, political actors at the time recognized that such a broad duty and right to wage war against perceived evildoers would be abused by kings and princes. To guard against this, in the thirteenth century Pope Innocent IV claimed that only the papacy had the authority to authorize wars against Christian princes or infidels who violated the natural law.[9] In other words, it was recognized that because a broad right to wage war in order to right wrongs could easily be abused, the authority to wage such wars should be taken out of the hands of those who might potentially abuse it.

During the second epoch, which ran from the end of the Middle Ages until 1945, the moral and legal consensus held that there was a right but not a duty to wage war to protect the innocent. Throughout this epoch there was a trend towards restricting that right until, by the eighteenth and nineteenth centuries, many liberals were arguing that no such right existed, while many states defended their legal rights to wage war if they saw fit. There were two important changes to the way that the right to wage war to protect the innocent was conceived: rights and duties were decoupled and – with the march of sovereignty and European expansion into the New World – the idea of a common Christian space was gradually replaced with one of separate and incommensurate political communities.

With the rebirth of colonization following the Spanish conquest of the Americas, writers such as Vitoria and Suárez began to tighten up the restrictions on the use of force to protect the innocent in order to guard against the abuse all too evident on the part of the Spanish conquistadors. They replaced the 'duty' to intervene with a 'permission' to do so and placed important limits on how the right could be invoked and on the scope of permissible action. Vitoria believed that humanity was a 'universal community' governed by natural law, but argued that the prosecution of war to protect the innocent be constrained. He pointed towards a *right* to protect the innocent but careful reading reveals that he did not think Christian rulers were *obliged* to do so. Given that all humans were created by God and were therefore all 'neighbours' in God's eyes, Vitoria argued that 'anyone, and especially princes *may* defend them from such tyranny and oppression'.[10] He singled out cannibalism and human sacrifice as providing just cause for war on similar grounds to the justification for a humanitarian war against terrorists. However, he insisted that princes may not continue to prosecute the war once the violations had ceased, may not use natural law as a pretext for seizing land or goods, conducting forcible conversions or despoiling Indians of wealth and gold, and must make provisions to protect those brought under their rule and increase their temporal goods, pass good laws, and ensure that they are enforced.[11]

Vitoria's successor, Suárez, accepted the idea that a state had just cause for war if the rights of either the state itself or its citizens were denied – though he was more reticent about granting princes permission to wage war to protect the rights of foreigners. Suárez argued – much as later liberals would – that governments were founded on the consent of their citizens.[12] They could not simply be overrun if they violated the natural rights of their citizens by terrorizing them or supporting the terrorism of others. Moreover, Suárez shared Vitoria's fear that granting princes a broad right to enforce natural law wherever it was violated could be abused since 'if the reasoning in question were valid, it would always be permissible to declare such a war on the ground of protecting innocent little children'.[13] He therefore insisted that the claim that sovereigns had authority to avenge injuries anywhere in the world was 'entirely false' because it would undermine international order, though he did admit that sovereigns may wage war when a ruler forced his subjects into idolatrous practices (which may include cannibalism and human sacrifice).[14]

The Thirty Years War in the seventeenth century marked an important watershed. It prompted Thomas Hobbes to argue that there was neither a community of humankind (a mainstay of earlier approaches) nor a society of states – a position we have come to associate with realism.[15] This view was rejected by Hugo Grotius, who developed a position very similar to Suárez's: that *in extremis* sovereigns have a right to aid the subjects of other states, but it is a limited right and there is no duty to do so. Grotius argued that all persons and states enjoy fundamental rights under natural law, which prohibited certain acts but did not demand that individuals aid one another.[16] He placed important limits on when sovereigns may wage war to aid others and remained deeply concerned about the potential for abuse. Nevertheless, Grotius rationalized that the potential for abuse does not undermine the veracity of the right:

> Hence, Seneca thinks that I may make war upon one who is not one of my people but oppresses his own ... a procedure which is often connected with the protection of innocent persons. We know, it is true, from both ancient and modern history, that the desire for what is another's seeks such pretexts as this for its own ends; but a right does not at once cease to exist in case it is to some extent abused by evil men. Pirates, also, sail the sea; arms are carried also by brigands.[17]

He insisted that subjects had a responsibility to obey the law, and were wrong to rebel in cases where their ruler was not obviously tyrannical. Even where rule was obviously tyrannical, Grotius refused to endorse a right of rebellion, though in such cases he did endorse the right of other sovereigns to intervene. Thus:

> The fact must also be recognized that kings, and those who possess rights equal to those kings, have the right of demanding punishments not only on account of injuries committed against themselves or their subjects, but also on account of injuries which do not directly affect them but excessively violate the law of nature or of nations in regard to any persons whatsoever.[18]

The two chief concerns evident in this work – that a state is based on the assumed consent of its citizens and the danger of abuse – coupled with the rise of the notion that humans could never fully know the objective justice of their cause, continued to erode the consensus on the right to defend foreigners against extreme violations of natural law such as terrorism. Still working within a broadly natural law framework, Pufendorf insisted that sovereigns did not have a right to punish others for violations of the natural law and may help third parties only when invited to do so.[19] Christian

Wolff removed even this caveat and imposed an absolute ban on 'punitive war', no matter how wicked a particular government might be.[20] The influential liberal John Stuart Mill endorsed this position, insisting that free governments could be established only through a domestic struggle for liberty. Mill shared Kant's view that a rule of non-intervention was a necessary prerequisite for free, republican government.[21]

The pre-eminent international lawyer of the eighteenth century, Emmerich de Vattel, bucked the trend. He certainly endorsed the general principle of non-intervention on the grounds that governments were established through the consent of their citizens:

> Nations and states are political bodies, societies of men who have united together and combined their force in order to protect their mutual advantage and security. It thus becomes a moral person which has understanding and will and is competent to undertake obligations and hold rights ... [thus] ... each citizen submits himself to the authority of the whole body.[22]

However, he accepted Pufendorf's view that intervention was permissible if a sovereign's rule was so tyrannical that it caused a revolt and the rebels requested aid.[23]

It is important to place these arguments in their proper historical context. The overriding concern for writers such as Hobbes and Grotius was to avoid a repetition of the disastrous wars that had engulfed Europe for much of the first half of the seventeenth century. War remained commonplace in Europe, but not until the twentieth century would it descend to the depths of the Thirty Years War. The post-Grotian writers mentioned above were galvanized by a mixture of concerns, but two stand out. First, there was a clear belief in the value of order predicated on an 'equalitarian' system of sovereign states, within Europe at least.[24] Second, liberals such as Pufendorf, Wolff and Mill were only too aware that a general right or duty to intervene on behalf of an ill-defined natural law would be used by absolutist monarchies to crush more liberal regimes.

Given this, it is not surprising that at the time an intellectual consensus was emerging in favour of either a complete ban on war for the purposes of protecting innocent foreigners or else a very limited right, European states themselves often justified their recourse to war by pointing to those very rights. In 1827 Russia and France used a mixture of humanitarian and religious arguments to justify their decision to intervene in Greece to prevent further Ottoman massacres of Greek Christians;[25] in 1860, a six-power protocol authorizing war to protect Christians in Syria insisted that 'the object of the mission is to assist stopping, by prompt and energetic measures, the effusion of blood and [to put] an end to the outrages committed against Christians, which cannot go unpunished';[26] in 1898 the US intervened in Spanish-ruled Cuba, citing among other things, 'the abhorrent conditions which … have shocked the moral sense of the people of the United States [and] have been a disgrace to Christian civilization'.[27] In a sense, all three interventions were attempts to use war to put an end to terrorist attacks by the governments in question.

International law caught up with the emerging consensus among philosophers only in 1945 – the beginning of the third epoch. At least three considerations helped to galvanize states into agreeing the blanket ban on the use of force described earlier. First, Hitler's use of humanitarian justifications to legitimize the invasion of Czechoslovakia demonstrated the danger of abuse all too clearly. Second, there was a widespread consensus that order could be maintained only if aggressive war was outlawed. Third, the anti-colonial movement insisted that foreign interference in the government of other nations was morally wrong. The post-1945 system did contain a mechanism for authorizing the use of force to protect people from terrorism in the form of the UN Security Council. Had the Council worked as intended and assumed responsibility for maintaining the peace, this mechanism might have provided a means for the collective prevention and punishment of grave violations of natural law (such as terrorism) while guarding against abuse.

But as we know only too well, the Security Council did not function as intended and its permanent members failed to assume their responsibilities as millions were killed in Biafra, Cambodia, Uganda, East Pakistan, Latin America, Zaire/ Democratic Republic of Congo, Rwanda, the Balkans, Afghanistan, East Timor and elsewhere. This litany of failure created a 'chasm' between the Security

Council's record and the professed aspirations of most of the world's peoples.[28] As a result there have been numerous attempts to articulate alternative approaches to the legitimization of force that circumvent the legal prohibition. Many draw upon the just war tradition and speak directly to the neoconservative agenda underpinning Bush's understanding of the war on terror.

For its part, the Catholic Church insists that individuals are members of both their state and the global 'human family'.[29] 'Solidarity', the Pope described as 'a firm and persevering determination to commit oneself to the common good ... because we are all really responsible for all'.[30] According to Richard Miller, this conception of solidarity creates a cosmopolitan ethos that views sovereignty as a relative value. In other words, current Catholic teaching holds that sovereignty is subordinate to individual rights.[31] As John Paul II put it, 'the principles of sovereignty of states and of non-interference in their internal affairs – which retain all their value – cannot constitute a screen behind which torture and murder can be carried out'.[32] From this perspective, sovereignty is seen as an instrumental value that enables governments to establish orderly and just societies but when governments fail to fulfil sovereignty's purpose, their legitimacy is diminished.[33] Because humanity is a unified whole, the use of force against sovereigns who support or indulge in terrorism is justified 'as an exercise of cosmopolitan justice or global solidarity'.[34]

To summarize, it is important to understand the moral and legal components of the debate about whether it is legitimate for a state to wage war to protect people from terrorism as intersecting streams rather than isolated traditions. The key dilemmas occur at those intersections when competing sets of values appear to pull in different directions. Is the ban on the use of force except in self-defence an instrumental or absolute value? Do individuals have fundamental rights that may never be breached? Do states have a duty and right to enforce common principles such as the principle that non-combatants not be deliberately targeted?

For our purposes, the most important aspect of this debate is the question of whether the violation of individual human rights in one part of the world creates a right for states in other parts of the world to intervene militarily. From the preceding discussion, there appears to be a wide consensus that there are common rights held by all that ought to be protected. Chief among these would be the right of a non-combatant not to be arbitrarily killed by terrorists. Only the most rigid of cultural relativists would argue that individuals have no inherent rights or that the right not to be arbitrarily killed by terrorists is not one of them – and there is none of those in the just war tradition.

If we can agree that there are fundamental rights that all individuals ought to enjoy, including protection from terrorism, then the debate about the broad definition of the war on terror offered at the beginning of this chapter boils down to the instrumental question of how best to realize those rights. For John Stuart Mill, those rights can be truly realized only by domestic struggles for liberation. That is, the people have to protect themselves against terrorism. Outside intervention, Mill would argue, would build only a weak barrier against terrorism. Others, however, argue that outsiders can play an important role in assisting the realization of rights, and the historical record from Germany and Japan to the Balkans today would seem to support this view. This then gets us to the heart of the problem – if we accept that terrorism violates universal rights and that external actors might justifiably intervene to protect those rights, which actors have the authority to uphold these common rights and in what circumstances?

At its heart, the issue that has divided just war theorists and international lawyers is the question of who has the authority to wage war to protect universal rights. Is it for a single sovereign to determine that the violation of rights by terrorism is so serious as to warrant the waging of war? If so, how do we arbitrate between different opinions among sovereigns, especially if a majority believe that terrorism does not warrant the waging of war? Given that the UN Security Council is the only entity legally empowered to author-ize wars other than wars of self-defence, is it the only appropriate authority to determine this matter? If a state wages a unilateral war on terror is it rendered immoral by the legitimate authority principle? Some prominent contemporary just war thinkers have criticized the UN Charter system for forbidding aggressive war and downplaying the role of justice in determining a war's legitimacy. According to

Johnson, for example, labelling a war as 'aggressive' does not resolve the question of whether it is just yet, he argues, the UN Charter makes precisely that presumption.[35] Likewise, Oliver O'Donovan argued that the legalism predominant in *jus ad bellum* be replaced by a 'praxis of judgment' that would permit war to end or prevent grave injustice regardless of its legal status, granting the just war tradition a 'natural law rather than positive law orientation'.[36] More pointedly, Elshtain called for a revived Augustinian account of the just war, permitting punishment (by war) of wrongdoers and perceiving the question of just cause in more or less objective terms.[37]

The main, and widely recognized, problem with the solution proposed by these prominent just war theorists – of simply rejecting international law when it comes to this question of authority – is the danger of abuse, a danger recognized by ethicists ever since the emergence of sovereign-style political entities. It is this danger, and the fear that relaxing the prohibition on force would make the world more violent and disorderly, that underpins the arguments of those who remain committed to the comprehensive prohibition on force. This is no idle fear. Over the past few decades, the prohibition on force and the multilateral peace regime engineered by the UN has presided over a steady and marked decline in the incidence of war and genocide and the lethality of war. Behind the headlines of a 'new world disorder' and the eruption of chaos and violence, the world is actually more peaceful today than a decade ago and where wars do erupt far fewer people are likely to be killed.[38] The fear is that those who would tear up this system by granting (some) states a right to wage unilateral war to protect people from the grave wrong that is terrorism would undermine this system, reversing the progress towards peace made in the past few decades. What is often overlooked, however, is that the UN Charter system offers a theoretical midpoint between total prohibition and an entirely permissive order by granting the Security Council the legal authority to authorize enforcement action.

As has long been recognized, there are very good reasons for denying sovereigns carte blanche to determine the legitimacy of their own cause. As the bitter experience of the Thirty Years War – and many wars since – attests, sovereigns are only too able to construct a just cause for themselves. How are we to know when a just cause is genuine? There are some cases where just cause is compelling. Some will be cases where a state has been subject to imminent or actual attack for no good reason, and this is the subject of the following chapter. There may, however, be clear-cut cases where the threat or wrong is so overwhelming as to permit governments to wage war unilaterally. But we should set a very high threshold, lest we open the door to potential abuse. In relation to the protection of non-combatants from terrorism, we would expect that only a widespread and systematic campaign of killing and/or forced displacement would warrant such unilateralism. The most obvious cases in this regard would be clear-cut cases of genocide – the use of terrorism to destroy an entire people – as in Rwanda in 1994. But the vast majority of cases – Iraq included – are far from this clear-cut. How are we to test the veracity of just cause claims in such instances?

This is where the UN Security Council comes in. The Council is a far from perfect body. It is unrepresentative, containing only fifteen members and omitting some of the world's largest states, such as India and Brazil, and some of its biggest economies, such as Japan and Germany (except when they are elected by the General Assembly to serve as non-permanent members). Its members quite obviously place their own national interests ahead of the common good that they are charged with protecting. And its activism is held hostage to the veto of the permanent five members. The veto, or threatened veto, has been used to block collective action in Kosovo and Darfur and condemnation of the Israeli mistreatment of some Palestinian non-combatants. It was even once used to block a resolution condemning Israel for attacking Red Cross vehicles. But, as I mentioned earlier, the veto plays a useful role in keeping the great powers engaged and ensuring that the UN does not act against their interests.

In relation to the interrogation of just causes, the UN Security Council acts as a sort of mini-court of world opinion and, to be fair, it often reflects world opinion better than we would like to think. For example, as much as I might not have liked it as a liberal defender of NATO's intervention in Kosovo, the Security Council's decision not to authorize that intervention reflected the majority of world opinion. Likewise with Iraq, the Security Council's position reflected world opinion. Around 150 of the world's 192 states opposed the war in Iraq. On the basis of this fact and opinion polling, it is fair to say that more than three-quarters of humanity believed the invasion of Iraq to be wrong. In both these cases, then, the Security Council was not inhibiting collective action on behalf of humanity but reflecting humanity's opposition to particular acts of war.

What was most interesting about the political and legal debate that preceded the invasion of Iraq was that the Security Council was treated as a de facto court of world opinion. The US repeatedly put forward its case for war there and the UN's weapons inspection team led by Hans Blix scrutinized some of the elements of that case. Blix supported some American suspicions (noting, for instance, that some anthrax was unaccounted for) and rejected others. The minutiae of the American case for war were scrutinized in and around the Security Council. Was Saddam seeking uranium from Niger? Did he have mobile chemical weapons laboratories? Were there ongoing chemical and biological weapons programmes? Did Iraq have connections to Al Qaeda terrorists? Did it pose a threat to its neighbours and the US? I will not dwell on the substance of this debate. My point is that the Security Council provided a forum to which the US and its allies brought their case for war and the rest scrutinized that case. In the end, as is well known, a majority of states in the Security Council found that the evidence presented did not provide just grounds for going to war with Iraq.

How does all of this relate back to our discussion of the war on terror? I would ask whether the war on terror is directed against a wrong so manifest, widespread and systematic that it may be prosecuted on the grounds of protecting the innocent and upholding fundamental rights without reference to either self-defence (the subject of the following chapter) or international authorization? I think the answer is no, precisely because the moniker 'war on terror' does not specify precisely which terrorists are targeted and on what grounds.

If we understand terrorism as the deliberate killing of non-combatants for political purposes and we presume that a 'war on terror' would pursue the worst offenders in this regard, then it would start not in the Middle East and Central Asia, but in Darfur and the Democratic Republic of Congo. It would not have singled out Saddam's regime as a terrorist government, but also North Korea, Burma, Sudan and many others whose records post-2001 were as bad – and in several cases much worse – than Saddam's. It might also have selected countries with better-established links to Al Qaeda – such as Pakistan and Saudi Arabia. In addition, it is far from clear that all terrorists commit wrongs so bad that they provide just cause for war. The so-called 'Real IRA' are terrorists and commit grave wrongs but there would be little support for the view that Britain would be justified in using the full weight of its military power against them. The same could be said of the Basque separatists in ETA and other such terrorist organizations. Thus, because the commission of terrorism itself – although always wrong – is not always sufficiently wrong to create grounds for war, it cannot be the case that a 'war on terror' is a just war. A war on certain terrorist groups or states might very well be just, but each war and each target needs to be scrutinized individually. The US and its allies could justify 3attacks on Afghanistan and Iraq by reference to self-defence but that requires a slightly different test and line of justification to the one offered by Bush at the beginning of the chapter. What is more, the self-defence argument only reinforces the need to identify precisely the targets of each individual military campaign, because we cannot act legitimately (or logically) in self-defence unless we can precisely specify the source of the threat. And we cannot act in self-defence against those who are not actually threatening us.

Why does all this matter so much? The reason was set out by those writers who confronted the turmoil of the Thirty Years War in Europe. If we allow sovereigns simply to satisfy themselves as to the justness of their cause, then the *jus ad bellum* restrictions become nothing more than a lexicon of self-justification – supporting and legitimizing war rather than controlling and limiting it. The consequence of this, we know from history, is a more violent and less just world. Great powers certainly have the material wherewithal to impose their version of justice, at least in the short term. But, as realists know only too well, a great power that does this creates animosity and encourages others to ally against it. In other words, acting contrary to shared international beliefs about appropriate behaviour exacts political and economic costs. Great powers are able to bear some of those costs, but not infinitely. To put it into a contemporary context, America's failure to sell its war in Iraq has left it with the military and economic burden of reconstruction. This is already having a significant impact on the American economy and levels of government debt. Even though it is often described as the 'greatest power the world has ever seen', America could not sustain a presence in Iraq while also assertively imposing its will on Iran and North Korea. To make matters worse, acting contrary to world opinion will only encourage our adversaries to ally against us.

It is important, therefore, that in cases where a government wishes to act to uphold universal rights, such as the right not to be killed by terrorists, by waging war on terrorists, it identifies which terrorists it wants to fight and its grounds for doing so. In some rare cases, the commission of terrorism may be so overwhelming that unilateralism can be justified, resulting in the systematic and widespread killing of non-combatants. In most cases, however, judgements about whether acts of terrorism provide sufficient just cause for war will be more borderline and it will be incumbent upon those who plan to wage war to persuade the court of world opinion of their case. The best proxy for that court is the Security Council. The Council may sometimes be blocked by a pernicious veto from a great power placing its own interests ahead of concern for the collective good. In cases where a majority of states (nine of the fifteen) support a case for war, but a resolution is blocked by veto we might say that there is a good moral, though not a legal, case for war. This is an appealing argument, but those tempted to make it need to bear in mind that the principle works both ways – it could, for example, be used to provide a moral override to a US veto on a matter relating to Israel.

A proportionate war?

Before I move on to discuss the question of self-defence in more detail it is worth looking at a second aspect of *jus ad bellum* that throws doubt on the legitimacy of the war on terror, namely proportionality. Recall that proportionality requires that the overall good to be achieved by a particular war outweighs the overall evil that it is expected to unleash. A leading American ethicist, Jean Bethke Elshtain, argued that the war on terror would be proportionate if the US and its allies avoided the use of weapons of mass destruction (WMD) and refrained from directly targeting civilians.[39] This view is, I think, fraught with difficulties, not only because it conflates (macro) proportionality with (micro) discrimination but also because it misses the elephant in the room – the fact that the justification for the war on terror does not specify who the terrorists are. I will briefly explore these questions in a little more depth.

First, as I noted in the previous section, given that 'terrorism' is a contested concept and that applying a morally consistent definition of terrorism as the deliberate killing of non-combatants would throw up countless examples of terrorism – both non-state and state – it is not clear that all those who are labelled terrorists provide proportionate grounds for war. As mentioned earlier, ETA and the Real IRA are clearly terrorists, yet waging all-out war against them would be disproportionate. Likewise, Russian forces in Chechnya waged war on the civilian population, levelling whole cities. This makes them terrorists; yet waging war against Russia would be a massively disproportionate response, likely to do far more harm than good.

Second, the war on terror is disproportionate because, ultimately, it is a war on a tactic, not a specific group of people. Terrorism is the deliberate killing of non-combatants for political purposes. There is no limit on the types of actors that could be terrorists. It is not at all clear how, exactly, one goes about waging war on a tactic. How often does the tactic have to be used for war to be a proportionate response? What is the objective of a war on terror? How do we know when it has succeeded – or is it an unending war? When Japan bombed Pearl Harbor, the US declared war on Japan – the source of the attack – not on 'surprise attacks' – the tactic used. Similarly, in relation to the war on terror, a proportionate (and logically coherent) response to the September 11 atrocities would have been to declare war on Al Qaeda and those groups allied to it that were engaging in violent confrontation with the US and its allies. If we do not know who our enemies are, we cannot wage a proportionate war against them.

Finally, the war on terror is disproportionate because by being so vague about its targets and objectives it can be used to justify actions that on closer inspection have very little to do with satisfying the just cause created by September 11. Thus, the invasion of Iraq, the doctrine of pre-emptive self-defence (see Chapter 4) and the policy of maritime interdiction, all of which were justified in terms of the war against terror, contributed nothing to realizing the just cause of defeating the perpetrators of 9/11 and defending America from attack. As such, it is hard to see how they were justifiable components of a war relating to 9/11.[40]

For these reasons, it seems fair to conclude that the war on terror cannot lay claim to being proportionate.

Conclusion

The idea of a war on terror may be inherently unjust, but that does not rule out the possibility that individual components of that war, such as the interventions in Afghanistan, Iraq, Yemen and Somalia, might be just. The point of this chapter has not been to argue that the use of force in response to terrorism is unjust but that the articulation of a global war on terror cannot be justified, primarily because its parameters are too broad. If governments are to do better in providing moral justifications for the recourse to force in relation to the war on terror, it is important to think of it not as one endless and seemingly limitless war but as a series of distinct and separate wars. Any military action designed to combat terrorism must either be a specific act of self-defence (see the following chapter) or must be directed against a sufficiently bad prior or imminently apprehended wrong.

When terrorists systematically attack non-combatants they violate moral principles that are common to all. In theory, such principles, enshrined in natural law or common morality, may be upheld by any public authority (not just the state directly threatened).[41] Individual states do not, however, have an unqualified legal or moral right to wage war. There is a wide body of law governing recourse to force that is reflective of international opinion, guards certain core values (such as the right to self-determination) and protects the just war criteria from potential abuse. In many situations, the justifiable use of force is compatible with the dominant view that there is a general legal ban on the use of force. There are two exceptions: self-defence and collective enforcement authorized by the Security Council. The right of self-defence is examined in the following chapter. However, it should be remembered that this right extends only to a right to wage war on groups and states that are actually engaged in an armed attack or are in the final stages of organizing such an attack. Either way, it requires that a source of threat be identified – and that the threat be actual or imminently apprehended.

The central problem examined in this chapter emerges out of the fact that the US has not limited itself to a defensive war but has advocated something more – a war aimed at the global eradication of terrorism, a war to protect the rights of civilians everywhere. But, in this case, the UN Security Council has refused to authorize collective action. This raises the question – in what situation is it morally justifiable to attack a group that targets non-combatants when those non-combatants are not one's own citizens or citizens of allies, and where the Security Council refuses to authorize collective action? The answer is dependent on the circumstances of each case. However, it seems clear that a case will be based on scale and grav-ity of the terrorism in question, and the more states the potential intervener is able to persuade of its case, the greater the legitimacy. The intervening state must demonstrate that the terrorists have systematically violated the rights of non-combatants; that the crisis is immediate and warrants the use of force to stem it; and that it is acting with 'right intent' – that is, the war is clearly directed against the 'terrorists' and has the restoration of peace as its primary aim. If these conditions are met, it is possible to envisage a situation where a war is launched against particular terrorists that is neither strictly speaking in self-defence nor authorized by the Security Council, but is none the less just. It is clear, however, that the current war on terror satisfies none of these conditions.

FOUR
Is pre-emption legitimate?

The right to use force in self-defence has been described as a 'fundamental principle' of international law and is also the bedrock of the just war tradition's just causes for war.[1] Traditionally, just war scholars have admitted that the right to self-defence comprises a right to respond with force to both actual and imminent attacks.[2] However, the ambiguous place of pre-emptive self-defence in Article 51 of the UN Charter gave rise to a debate between traditionalists, who advocate a literal interpretation of the Charter (thus ruling out the use of force prior to an armed attack) and those who argue that the UN Charter does not override a right of pre-emptive self-defence that existed before the Charter was established.

As is well known, these debates have become more pointed in the wake of 9/11, as the right of pre-emption has become a cornerstone of America's strategy in the war on terror. In the wake of those attacks, many scholars and policy-makers began to insist that the ability of terrorists and 'rogue states' to inflict mass casualties at short notice required a less restrictive way of thinking about self-defence. The so-called 'Bush doctrine' claimed a right for the US to act pre-emptively against terrorists, states harbouring terrorists and other 'rogue' regimes. For some, it amounted to claiming an 'unlimited' right of self-defence.[3]

This chapter takes up the challenge to re-examine the right of self-defence in the wake of September 11. It accepts the view that self-defence needs to be rethought to take account of the fact that massive threats may emerge more rapidly and quietly than before. Though appealing for its simplicity, the traditional view that there is, and should be, no right of pre-emptive self-defence against terrorists and those harbouring them is discounted on at least two counts.[4] First, a 'right' of self-defence that does not permit states to use force to pre-empt attacks is not much of a right. Second, in the contemporary context, denying the global hyperpower the right to pre-empt attacks is likely only to encourage that power to reject the normative restraints on recourse to force. But there are also good reasons for avoiding an entirely permissive order, as a permissive rule of self-defence could encourage states to abuse that right and would blur the distinction between aggression and defence so critical to *jus ad bellum*.[5]

This chapter aims to develop a new way of thinking about pre-emptive self-defence to take account of the threat of terrorism. It begins by outlining the moral and legal rules relating to self-defence and continues by suggesting a new conception of pre-emption and showing how this might shape our moral assessment of the use of force against Yemen and Iraq, two hotly contested instances of pre-emption in the war on terror.

Self-defence in the just war tradition

It is quite uncontroversial to argue for self-defence as the primary just cause for war. Indeed, for many prominent just war thinkers, sovereigns had not only a right but also a *duty* to defend their communities. As Vattel put it, 'self-defence against an unjust attack is not only a right which every nation has, but it is a duty, and one of the most sacred duties'.[6] Both Suarez and Wolff supported this view.[7] This obligation derived from the sovereign's responsibility to protect his or her subjects.

There was a similar level of consensus about pre-emptive self-defence. On the whole, just war thinkers tended to permit a limited right of pre-emption in the face of an imminent threat but expressly rejected the preventive war, viewing it as tantamount to aggression. Grotius listed as the first 'just cause' of war:

> an injury not yet done which menaces body or goods ... [In cases where one is] menaced by present force with danger of life not otherwise evitable, war is lawful, even to the slaying of the aggressor ... as a matter of self-protection.[8, 9]

This right, however, was limited by necessity: 'the right of self-defence exists only when necessary: where the danger can be avoided, delay is proper to allow recourse to other remedies'.[10] The danger,

Grotius argued, must be 'immediate and imminent in point of time'.[11] Lest there be any doubt about the limits of this right, Grotius went on specifically to reject the legality of preventive war as an 'intolerable doctrine'.[12]

Samuel Pufendorf agreed that a man may kill an aggressor if:

> the aggressor, showing clearly his desire to take my life, and equipped with the capacity and the weapons for his purpose ... has gotten into the position where he can in fact hurt me.[13]

Like Grotius, Pufendorf also sought to limit the right, insisting that force could be used only in the absence of viable alternatives (such as escape).[14]

Vattel was a little more permissive than the others, insisting that:

> When once a state has given proofs of injustice, rapacity, pride, ambition, or an imperious thirst of rule, she becomes an object of suspicion to her neighbours, whose duty it is to stand on their guard against her ... [O]n occasions where it is impossible or too dangerous to wait for an absolute certainty, we may justly act on a reasonable presumption.[15]

However, he insisted that if there were reasonable doubts about these proofs, a state should take care 'not to act upon vague and doubtful suspicions lest it should run the risk of becoming itself the aggressor'.[16] Although Vattel accepted the idea that a state may pre-emptively attack another without knowing for certain that the other is close to attacking it, he expressly forbade preventive war. The fact that a state increases its power was not enough grounds for war, Vattel argued, because 'we must have good grounds to think ourselves threatened ... before we can have recourse to arms'.[17]

This view was broadly reflected in international law prior to 1945. The 1928 Kellogg–Briand pact, whose signatories renounced the use of force in their international relations, nevertheless reserved the right to use force in self-defence. That right, it was widely conceded, included the right to pre-emption. According to Frank Kellogg, the US Secretary of State who co-wrote the pact, the right of self-defence is:

inherent in every sovereign state and is implicit in every treaty. Every nation is free at all times and regardless of treaty provisions to defend its territory from attack or invasion and it alone is competent to decide whether circumstances require recourse to war in self-defence.[18]

The just war tradition and international law after 1945 make very similar demands when it comes to the question of pre-emptive self-defence. Article 51 of the UN Charter gives states an inherent right of self-defence. It declares that:

> Nothing in the present Charter shall impair the inherent right of individual or collective self-defence if an armed attack occurs against a member of the United Nations, until the Security Council has taken measures necessary to maintain international peace and security. Measures taken by members in the exercise of this right shall be immediately reported to the Security Council and shall not in any way affect the authority and responsibility of the Security Council under the present Charter to take at any time such action as it deems necessary in order to maintain or restore international peace and security.

It is worth noting that in the French version of this article, the phrase 'inherent right' is rendered '*droit naturel*' (natural right), a clear indication of the close links between international law and natural moral law.[19]

Since 1945, legal interpretations of Article 51 have tended to fall into one of two camps, divided by two issues in particular: what constitutes an 'armed attack' and do states have a right to act pre-emptively? Traditionalists argue for a narrow interpretation of the Charter on both counts.[20] The question of what constitutes an armed attack was first raised in 1948 when the USSR intervened in Czechoslovakia to overthrow a government that wished to participate in the Marshall Plan. Despite Czechoslovak pleas to the contrary, the Security Council did not see this intervention as an 'armed attack'. Likewise, in the same year, while the UN sent monitors to observe alleged border incursions by Yugoslav communists into Greece, it stopped short of identifying an armed attack.[21] These experiences led traditionalists to claim that an 'armed attack' was limited to cases of actual invasion and not limited incursions. This view was supported by the International Court of Justice in its judgment in the *Nicaragua vs US* case (1986). While finding that the sending of armed bands into another state may constitute an armed attack, the Court insisted that it was 'necessary to distinguish the most grave forms of the use of force (those constituting an armed attack) from other less grave forms'.[22] Traditionalists therefore argue that an armed attack should be understood as being limited to those instances involving the direct use of conventional military force. According to this view, in cases of sabotage or state-sponsored terrorism the victim state does not enjoy a right to use force against the host state in self-defence.[23]

Traditionalists maintain that Article 51 expressly rules out preemptive self-defence, insisting that states have a right to use force in self-defence only *after* an armed attack has occurred. In the *Nicaragua vs US* case, the International Court of Justice supported this interpretation. It ruled that:

> for one state to use force against another ... is regarded as lawful, by way of exception, only when the wrongful act provoking the response was an armed attack ... In the view of the Court, under international law in force today – whether customary international law or that of the United Nations system – states do not have a right of 'collective' armed response to acts which do not constitute an 'armed attack'.[24]

Thus Hans Kelsen concluded that Article 51 applied only 'in case of an armed attack' and that the right could not be exercised to protect states against the violation of any of their other rights.[25]

Although there is evidence that the Charter's drafters intended Article 51 to provide only a limited right of self-defence, the idea that a state should wait to be attacked before taking measures to defend its citizens has been widely criticized – and for good reason. Sir Humphrey Waldock insisted that:

> it would be a travesty of the purposes of the Charter to compel a defending state to allow its assailant to deliver the first, and

perhaps fatal blow … to read Article 51 literally is to protect the aggressor's right to the first strike.[26]

Many scholars therefore insist that Article 51 does not override the customary rights identified at the beginning of this section – including a right to pre-emption.

This approach holds that the definition of an 'armed attack' should be understood more broadly and that Article 51 does not erode a state's right to pre-emptive self-defence. On the first issue, these scholars insist that if the phrase 'armed attack' means what it says, it must therefore mean all 'armed attacks' regardless of their scale.[27] Once again, in the *Nicaragua vs US* case the International Court of Justice put forward a traditional view, arguing that the provision of arms, logistics and other support to terrorists did not constitute an 'armed attack'. Many governments and legal scholars disagreed. For them, state support for terrorism constitutes an armed attack so long as the level of violence reaches (or threatens to reach) what the General Assembly's 'Definition of Aggression' labelled 'sufficient gravity'.[28]

This approach also insists that Article 51 does not diminish a state's inherent right to pre-emptive self-defence. There are at least two justifications for this view. First, that it is implied in the Charter's language. Article 51 explicitly endorses a state's *inherent* right to self-defence; in the French version its *natural* right. That inherent right clearly includes a right to pre-emptive self-defence, supporters of this approach argue. Moreover, if Article 51 is read as permitting the use of force against breaches of Article 2 (4) – the article banning the use of force, then this also permits pre-emption because Article 2 (4) prohibits both the 'threat' and 'use' of force.[29]

The second justification for a broader reading of Article 51 is customary practice. Since 1945, states have tended to judge instances of pre-emptive self-defence on the merits of each case.[30] On some occasions, where the threat is demonstrably imminent, governments have shown themselves willing to tolerate pre-emption. The paradigmatic case of this was the world's reaction to Israel's 1967 pre-emptive attack on Egypt. In that case, although some states condemned Israel, many others accepted that an Egyptian invasion was imminent and while desisting from commending Israel also chose not to condemn it.[31]

As I will show in the next section, Operation Enduring Freedom provides a compelling case in which the overwhelming majority of states supported the US's right to overthrow the Taliban regime in Afghanistan in order to pre-empt further Al Qaeda attacks. In other cases, however, states have been criticized as precipitating the use of force for ostensibly pre-emptive purposes. For example, when Israel launched an air strike against the Osirak nuclear reactor in Iraq in 1981, it was 'strongly condemned' by the UN Security Council even though several international lawyers supported Israel's case.[32] States found that the reactor did not pose an imminent threat and that Israel had resorted to force as a first, not last, resort.[33] What this demonstrates is that states and scholars are prepared to make judgements about the legitimacy of pre-emptive force on a case-by-case basis, lending support to the claim that there is a theoretical right of pre-emption in certain circumstances.

It seems clear from this that the right of self-defence permits the pre-emptive use of force in certain exceptional cases but forbids 'preventive' attacks. But in what situations is the pre-emptive use of force justifiable? And where do we draw the line between pre-emption and prevention? We can begin to answer these questions by considering the exchange of diplomatic notes between the UK and US concerning the sinking of the *Caroline* in 1837.

In 1837, the UK and US were in a state of peace. However, there was an armed insurrection (the 'Mackenzie rebellion') against British rule in Canada. The rebels began using an American-owned ship, the *Caroline*, to supply the rebels from the American side of the Niagara River. On 29 December 1837, Canadian troops loyal to Britain boarded the ship, killed several Americans, set the ship alight and allowed it to drift over the Niagara Falls. At the time of the attack the *Caroline* was docked on the US side of the border, not in its usual port on the Canadian side. The US protested against the attack, claiming that it violated its sovereignty, but the British insisted they were exercising their right to self-defence.

The debate began with a note from US Secretary of State John Forsyth to the British Minister in Washington on 5 January 1838.[34]

Forsyth demanded a full explanation from the British and labelled the attack an 'extraordinary outrage'. The British Minister responded by blaming the Americans for failing to prevent the use of its territory by the Canadian rebels and justifying the attack as 'a necessity of self-defence and self-preservation' against the 'piratical' vessel.[35] On further investigation in London, the British government concluded that as the *Caroline* was aiding and abetting the rebels, it was a legitimate target regardless of which side of the border it was docked. Not surprisingly, the US rejected this argument, disputing both the labelling of the *Caroline* as 'piratical' and Britain's claim to a right of 'hot pursuit' across the border. Instead, it argued that the level of threat that could justify hot pursuit must be 'imminent, and extreme, and involving impending destruction'.[36]

In late 1840, a former British soldier was arrested in New York and charged with arson and murder in relation to the *Caroline*. The US government invited the British to apologize for the incident and pay compensation in return for the dismissal of charges against the soldier. The British Minister agreed immediately and despatched a note of apology to the US government. In an 1842 reply, the American Secretary of State Daniel Webster explained that for the claim of self-defence to be justifiable, Britain was required to 'show a necessity of self-defence, instant, overwhelming, leaving no choice of means, and no moment for deliberation'.[37] The action taken must also involve 'nothing unreasonable or excessive; since the act, justified by the necessity of self-defence, must be limited by that necessity and kept clearly within it'.[38] In order to invoke a right of pre-emptive self-defence, therefore, a state has to demonstrate the imminence of an attack, the necessity of pre-emption and the proportionality of its intended response. Interestingly, Webster argued that the principles of necessity and proportionality were the most important and went into some detail in explaining what necessity entailed:

It must be demonstrated that it [Britain] did nothing unreasonable or excessive; since the act justified by the necessity of self-defence, must be limited by that necessity, and kept clearly within it.
It must be shown that admonition or remonstrances to the persons on board the Caroline was impracticable or would have been

unavailing; it must be shown that daylight could not be waited for; that there could be no discrimination, between the innocent and the guilty; that it would not have been enough to seize and detain the vessel; but that it was a necessity, present and inevitable.[39]

The *Caroline* case helps to overcome the political problems caused by Article 51's insistence that a right of self-defence can be claimed only *after* an armed attack has taken place. However, in light of Article 51, state practice since 1945 and the position taken by the International Court of Justice, the three cornerstones of the Webster formula – imminence, necessity and proportionality – at best constitute a limited right of pre-emptive self-defence.[40] There are therefore good grounds for arguing that contemporary international law permits a limited right of pre-emptive self-defence that extends beyond Article 51.

Between them, therefore, just war morality and international law grant states a limited right of pre-emptive self-defence in cases that satisfy the usual *jus ad bellum* criteria (all recourse to force must satisfy those criteria) plus the criteria of imminence (the attack must be demonstrably imminent) and necessity (the use of force must be the only reasonable measure available). According to this view, acts that do not satisfy all these criteria are illegal and unjust. Jurists worry, with good reason, that expanding the right beyond that of the *Caroline* formula would significantly increase the likelihood of abuse by states and make it harder for observers to evaluate the legitimacy of a state's claims. For instance, if we remove the obligation for a state to demonstrate than an attack is imminent, it becomes impossible to judge whether the claim to be acting in self-defence is valid.

The problem, however, comes in defining what 'imminence' means if the threat comes from terrorists and rogue states that possess the ability to launch instant mass casualty attacks on urban centres. As George W. Bush put it, in the post-September 11 context:

We have every reason to assume the worst, and we have an urgent duty to prevent the worst from happening … [we] cannot wait for the final proof – the smoking gun – that could come in the form of a mushroom cloud.[41]

This fear cannot be dismissed lightly and it is for this reason that we have to pose the question of whether the traditional doctrine of self-defence continues to hold up in the face of terrorist threats that call the concepts of 'imminence' and 'necessity' into doubt.

Pre-empting terrorism?

In light of what we now know about how far terrorists are prepared to go, there are at least four good reasons to rethink pre-emptive self-defence. First, on prudential grounds, there is an argument that prevention is better than cure. In hindsight, Clinton's decision not to take firmer action against Osama bin Laden between 1996 and 1998 was a bad misjudgement.[42] By this logic, the norm of pre-emptive self-defence must be refashioned to place fewer costs on political leaders who wish to take earlier action against would-be terrorists. Second, whereas conventional wars are preceded by clear warnings – most obviously troop mobilizations and deployments – such indicators do not usually precede mass casualty terrorist attacks.[43] It is virtually impossible for a liberal democracy to guard against terrorism at all times and in all places. There is widespread agreement, therefore, that the best way to reduce the threat of terrorism is to take the offensive and adopt a proactive strategy.[44] Third, the potential for mass casualty terrorism renders a reactive strategy imprudent at best. If one accepts Vattel's insistence that self-defence is the sacred duty of sovereigns, adopting a reactive strategy in the face of such a threat may even be immoral. Finally, although deterrence still has an important role to play in world politics – particularly in relation to so-called 'rogue states' – its ability to constrain the type of terrorism witnessed on September 11 in the short term is limited.

In its 2002 *National Security Strategy*, the US government offered a new and controversial avenue for rethinking pre-emptive self-defence. It was predicated on the view put forward by Donald Rumsfeld that:

> [T]he problem with terrorism is that there is no way to defend against the terrorists at every place and every time against every conceivable technique. Therefore, the only way to deal with the terrorist network is to take the battle to them.[45]

The *Strategy* insisted that:

> [G]iven the goals of rogue states and terrorists, the United States
> can no longer solely rely on a reactive posture as we have in the
> past. The inability to deter a potential attacker, the immediacy of
> today's threat, and the magnitude of potential harm that could be
> caused by our adversaries' choice of weapons, do not permit that
> option. We cannot let our enemies strike first.[46]

Despite the vociferous global opposition it incited, the *Strategy* advocated neither a radical reformulation of the law nor rule-breaking
behaviour. Instead, it situated the new doctrine firmly within customary international law and argued for the revision of one of the
three elements of Webster's test outlined during the *Caroline* affair:
imminence. Thus, it insisted that, 'for centuries, international law
recognized that nations need not suffer an attack before they can
lawfully take action to defend themselves'.[47] However, it maintained
that the concept of 'imminent threat' was in need of reform to
permit action 'even if uncertainty remains as to the time and place
of the enemy's attack. To forestall or prevent such hostile acts by our
adversaries, the United States will, if necessary, act pre-emptively.'[48]
This approach was justified because the US could not wait until a
terrorist threat was 'fully formed'.[49]

The *Strategy* has been widely criticized for stretching the concept
of 'armed attack' to such an extent that it loses any legal meaning
and for being deliberately misleading in labelling what is in essence a
strategy of *prevention* as pre-emption.[50] However, the problem is not
so much what the *Strategy* itself says, but with the Bush administration's rhetoric and actions. Indeed, a few states, including Russia
and India, responded favourably to the *Strategy* document.[51] There
is, however, an important disjuncture between the *Strategy* and US
rhetoric. Recall that the *Strategy* permits doubt only about the time
and place of the attack. According to this document, the enemy
target must still be shown to have both the *intent* to attack and the
means of doing so. Bush's rhetoric has been much less nuanced. In
a speech to the German parliament in May 2002 Bush argued that
the US would be prepared to use force against 'rogues', whether or
not those rogues had displayed a specific intent to attack the US or

its allies and *before* they acquired the means of doing so.[52] A month later, he told a West Point graduation ceremony that 'we must take the battle to the enemy and confront the worst threats before they emerge' telling the graduates to prepare for 'pre-emptive action'.[53] In its public statements, therefore, the US administration has certainly implied that it supports a right of preventive war, not the more limited right of expanded pre-emption claimed in the *Strategy*. According to the rhetoric a potential target need possess neither an intention nor the means of attacking the US and its allies.

The efforts of the Bush administration to justify the 2003 invasion of Iraq as an act of pre-emptive self-defence have helped solidify the view that the US has actually adopted a strategy of prevention. The US administration was clearly divided on the issue. When asked whether Iraq was an example of the strategy in practice, Secretary of State Colin Powell emphatically replied 'no, no, no'.[54] Instead, Powell preferred to argue that the war was justifiable because it was implicitly authorized by UN Security Council resolutions. However, Vice-President Dick Cheney repeatedly justified the war in terms of the need to *prevent* Iraq acquiring weapons of mass destruction (WMD) and since the war Bush himself has fallen back on the argument that 'America is safer' as a result.[55]

Thus, although the *Strategy* itself offers a reasonable starting point for rethinking the concept of pre-emptive self-defence, it is important to bear in mind that in both its rhetoric and practice the Bush administration deviated considerably from it and equated prevention with pre-emption. How, then, should pre-emptive self-defence be reconceptualized to meet the threat of terrorism? First of all it should be noted that the expanded concept of pre-emptive self-defence offered here applies only to the threat of terrorism as defined in Chapter 2 (be that from states or non-state actors).

The two central concepts of pre-emptive self-defence are 'imminence' and 'necessity'. According to the US *Strategy*, it is only the former that needs rethinking. Traditionally, both international law and just war morality have defined 'imminence' in temporal terms. A threat is imminent only immediately before the hammer falls. An attack is imminent when the enemy has displayed an intention to attack, has armed itself, has deployed its forces into an offensive formation and is about to strike. The problem is that if the planned attack is a mass casualty terrorist attack, it is usually too late to respond at this point. It is therefore unreasonable to expect a government to wait this long before taking forcible measures to prevent an expected attack. In this regard, we cannot overlook the fact that the existence of such a tight definition of imminence derived from the *Caroline* case may be due, at least in part, to some of the specificities of that case – the two parties to the dispute were liberal states with reasonably good relations.[56] In cases where mutual mistrust is considerably higher – and doubt and mistrust are seldom higher than when confronting mass casualty terrorism – a wider concept of imminence ought to be conceded to provide states with realistic means of preventing terror attacks against their citizens.

It is fair to conclude that in situations where a state can demonstrate an actor has the intention and means to conduct terrorist attacks against its citizens or its allies, it is reasonable to suggest that the imminence test is satisfied. The *demonstrability* of the intent and the means is critical, however. As I argued in the previous chapter, it is not enough for a government to convince itself of the threat. It must present reliable and accurate evidence to its own citizens, other states and global civil society.[57] Others will evaluate the evidence to decide whether, on a case-by-case basis, a particular pre-emptive attack was legitimate by reference to the demonstrable gravity of the threat, the known intentions of the potential terrorists and their ability to satisfy those intentions. In some cases it is not appropriate for a state to reveal what it knows *before* it launches a pre-emptive attack because doing so risks informing the terrorists of what it knows and losing the opportunity to strike them, but the burden of proof falls squarely on those that use pre-emptive force to demonstrate their case either before or immediately afterwards.[58]

The second criterion that must be satisfied is necessity. As stated above, according to Webster, necessity required that the threat being tackled be 'instant, overwhelming, leaving no choice of means and no moment for deliberation'. State practice has recognized that this sets the bar too high. Neither Israel's 1967 attack on Egypt nor the 2001 invasion of Afghanistan by the US and its allies would satisfy these criteria. Writing in 1961, McDougal and Feliciano offered a more appropriate understanding of necessity. For them, the necessity criterion is satisfied when the degree of imminence is 'so high as to preclude effective resort by the intended victim to non-violent modalities of response'.[59] Pre-emptive self-defence is warranted when the use of force is the only reasonable way in which the threat can be averted. It does not require that all other means be exhausted first, but we are entitled to ask whether those who use pre-emptive force had reasonable alternatives. For instance, in most, though not all, instances of pre-emptive attacks against terrorists we might expect the state using force to explore options beforehand with the state in whose territory it is using force. At the very least, we would expect a government using pre-emptive force in this way to be able to demonstrate that it seriously considered other, non-violent options and for it to explain its reasons for not choosing these other courses of action.

Although this expanded concept of pre-emption helps to meet the strategic challenge posed by terrorism, it creates three potential problems that international law attempted to overcome by outlawing the use of force and tightly limiting the scope of the right to self-defence. The first is the problem of abuse that raised its head in the previous chapter. Making the concept of pre-emptive self-defence more flexible can blur important moral distinctions and create avenues for political leaders to justify aggressive wars in terms of pre-emption. Henry Kissinger, for example, observed in relation to the *National Security Strategy* that 'it cannot be either in American national interests or the world's interest to develop principles that grant every nation an unfettered right of pre-emption against its own definition of threats to its security'.[60] In other words, an expansive right of self-defence could grant enough leeway for states to justify almost any use of force, making the world more, not less, danger-ous. The principal barrier to abuse in the schema offered here is accountability. Governments are obliged to demonstrate their case to their own citizens, other states and global civil society. If they fail in persuading these constituencies of their case, they cannot claim to be acting legitimately.

The second problem is that by adding further ambiguity to the application of the right of pre-emptive self-defence this revised doctrine places greater moral weight on the factual elements of each case. Assessments of factual evidence are never free of values and politics and an emphasis on facts gives the powerful an opportunity to sway others by bringing financial, military and political pressure to bear. As Michael Byers argues, this means that 'it is more likely that the criterion of imminence would be regarded satisfied when the United States wished to act militarily than when others wished to do the same'.[61]

It is certainly the case that weak states, and states that are out of favour in the West, would have a much more difficult time persuading the world's great powers of their cause than would the US and its allies. That is not to say that American claims will always be generally accepted, however, as the Iraq case demonstrates only too well. The powerful certainly have much more room for manoeuvre than the weak, but that is true of the ethics of war itself and of every aspect of international life – the more powerful you are, the more you can get away with. But, as I argued in the previous chapter, power does not grant limitless freedom of action. Perceived rule breaking always imposes costs and although the powerful are better able to bear those costs than the weak, at least in the short term, in the longer term the accumulation of costs can become unbearable, even for the strongest world powers.

The third problem is that a more permissive doctrine of self-defence may significantly increase the potential for error.[62] In a more permissive normative context, states may be encouraged to use force precipitately, based on flawed intelligence or misperceptions about threat – as a charitable interpretation of the decision to invade Iraq might suggest. There are no sure ways of eliminating this problem. It stands to reason that the earlier a state acts to pre-empt a perceived threat the more likely the chances for error and misperception, and vice-versa: a state that waits longer will be more certain of its case but risks waiting too long. The problem can be moderated but not resolved by the requirement of *demonstrability*, which insists that the more perspectives that are brought to bear on a particular problem, the less likely are the chances of error and misperception. A government is required to be sure of its case when it acts pre-emptively and it must demonstrate that it has taken every reasonable step to verify its evidence by taking alternative perspectives and evidence into account. If a state fails to demonstrate due care, it acts unjustly.

It is therefore important to limit this expanded right to pre-emptive self-defence. The expanded right proposed here is limited to cases where the anticipated threat is terrorist. There are no good grounds for reforming the traditional concept of self-defence in response to perceived conventional threats from so-called 'rogue states'. To claim the expanded right, a state must satisfy the *jus ad bellum* criteria plus the revised requirements of imminence and necessity outlined above. On top of all that, a state claiming this right must make itself accountable by presenting its case for others to evaluate either before or immediately after the pre-emptive attack and it must be able to demonstrate that it has shown due care in order to reduce the likelihood of error or misperception.

To sum up: the expanded right of pre-emption poses only two tests – imminence and necessity. To satisfy the first test, those invoking the expanded right must demonstrate that a group or state has both the intention and the means to conduct terrorist attacks. However, unlike the traditional concept, under the expanded concept it is not necessary to know with certainty precisely when or where the terrorists will strike. To satisfy the second requirement, the state using force pre-emptively must demonstrate that its use is necessary: that is, the use of force is the only way that the threat can be neutralized. The final section will consider how this framework can help us reach moral judgements about pre-emption.

Yemen

On 3 November 2002, a Predator drone belonging to the CIA launched two Hellfire missiles that destroyed a car travelling along a desert road in Yemen, close to the border with Saudi Arabia.[63] The Pentagon claimed that the target was Qaed Salim Sinan al-Harethi, the head of Al Qaeda's operations in Yemen and thought to be the mastermind behind the 2000 attack on the *USS Cole*.[64]

The US used three types of justification for the attack – suggesting that it was not too sure about the moral and legal basis of its actions. This was a justificatory strategy that was repeated in relation to

Iraq and gave the impression that offering a number of more or less plausible justifications amounted to a single good justification. First, it argued that the attack did not raise *jus ad bellum* issues because it was simply another addition to the global 'war on terror'.[65] As Condoleezza Rice explained, 'we're in a new kind of war, and we've made very clear that it is important that this new kind of war be fought on different battlefields'.[66] In other words, the battlefield for the war on terror is global and the violence unconventional and intermittent.[67] There are many problems with this position, which were canvassed in the previous chapter. In short, to reiterate the point made in Chapter 3, one cannot wage – either morally or logically – a 'war on terrorism' without specifying precisely whom it is one is combating and offering *jus ad bellum* justifications for the use of force. The fact that the US took its campaign to another state, endangering Yemeni non-combatants, means that we are entitled to explore the *jus ad bellum* question of whether it was a legitimate act of pre-emptive self-defence. Not least, as Mary Ellen O'Connell argues, we are entitled to ask these questions because at the time of the attack Yemen was not itself engaged in an armed conflict.[68] There is a danger that granting the US a right to strike anywhere at any time in the name of the 'war on terror' risks undermining the *jus ad bellum* constraints on the recourse to force. Such an approach gives rise to the belief that the US is not bound by conventional rules – a view often aired by members of America's political elite. As Warren Rudman, a former US senator and chair of the President's Foreign Intelligence Advisory Board during the Clinton administration put it, 'in the war on terror there are no rules. They [the terrorists] have none and you have to take whatever risks you have to take to make them fear us.'[69]

The second justification offered was that the Yemeni government had given its consent. According to some reports, Yemeni authorities were responsible for providing the US with the necessary intelligence to enable it to strike.[70] This claim certainly covers potential legal concerns about the strike, because the right of a state to request assistance from other states to suppress terrorist groups is widely recognized.[71] However, it does not resolve the moral questions because of the possibility that Yemen's consent may have been

coerced – and there is a history to the American–Yemeni relationship. In 1990 Yemen voted against Resolution 678 authorizing the
use of force to eject Iraqi forces from Kuwait. In response, the US
cut its financial assistance to Yemen by almost 90 per cent.[72] It is
therefore possible that Yemen's consent was coerced, though there is
not enough evidence to decide the matter either way. All we need to
say here is to reiterate that while host state consent certainly eases
the legal difficulties, it does not resolve the moral question – because
there is no reason to think that the Yemeni government is incapable
of consenting to an immoral military action.

The third justification did engage with *jus ad bellum*. The US
also insisted that the strike was an act of pre-emptive self-defence
against a known Al Qaeda leader who had targeted the US before
and was, in all probability, planning to do so again. Former Deputy
Defense Secretary, Paul Wolfowitz, described the attack as a successful tactical operation that had removed a danger to the US.[73]
Similarly, John Aldicott insisted that the attack was a legitimate act
of self-defence against enemy combatants.[74]

In order to evaluate the claim that the missile strike was a
legitimate act of self-defence we need to apply the expanded concept
of pre-emptive self-defence outlined earlier because the perceived
threat was genuinely terrorist in nature. We need to ask whether the
threat was imminent in the expanded sense of the term, whether
the use of force was necessary and whether the US displayed due
care. The answer to the first question is relatively straightforward.
The intended target, Harethi, was believed to be a leading member
of the Al Qaeda cell that targeted the *USS Cole* in 2000. If that is
the case, it is fair to conclude that the imminence test was satisfied
because Harethi had a clearly expressed intention to strike the US
and – presumably – the means to do so once again at some point.

This focus on the identity of the intended target raises the question of how sure we are that Harethi *was* in fact who the US claimed
he was. After all, in the light of the Iraqi WMD issue there are good
reasons for not taking US intelligence at face value. This in turn
raises the question of what standard of proof we require. Many
of the attack's critics complained that the US was acting as judge,
jury and executioner and that by taking pre-emptive action rather

than arresting and trying the suspects it failed to prove Harethi's guilt 'beyond reasonable doubt'.[75] Asa Kasher, for instance, argues that pre-emptive strikes against individuals can be justified only in cases where it is almost certain that the individual will launch a terrorist attack and there is no other reasonable way of preventing it.[76] However, in light of the previous discussion it could be fairly argued that this formula sets the threshold too high, because it is difficult to know with certainty precisely when and where a terrorist will strike. For guidance, we might turn to the First Geneva Protocol (1977) which insists in relation to targeting that the principle of 'due care' requires combatants to take 'every feasible precaution' to minimize harm to non-combatants. From Vitoria onwards, the just war tradition has accepted the idea that we can never be certain about the just causes for going to war and, I think, it is unreasonable to expect states combating terrorism to apply a higher standard of proof. So, given the evidence supplied by the US and apparently corroborated by Yemen, and the fact that no plausible counter-evidence has emerged, it is fair to conclude that Harethi did pose a threat and that measures against him were therefore justified.

To satisfy the second component of the expanded concept of self-defence offered here – necessity – the US needs to demonstrate that there were no reasonable alternatives to the use of force. Some of the attack's critics, including Amnesty International, focused on the question of whether the US and Yemen could have arrested the suspects and subjected them to due process.[77] Amnesty wrote to the administration asking whether the US and Yemen had attempted to arrest the suspects before using force.[78] Since the attack, no evidence has emerged to suggest that either Yemen or the US seriously contemplated arresting the suspects. Back in December 2001, however, thirteen Yemeni soldiers had been killed in an operation aimed at arresting Harethi and destroying Al Qaeda cells near the Saudi border.[79] Although the US strike came almost one year later, it is at least plausible to argue that it was part of an ongoing campaign against Al Qaeda in Yemen. Having failed with conventional means, this line of argument goes, the Yemeni government and the US were entitled to utilize alternative strategies. This is a plausible justification because law enforcement officers, like soldiers, are not required to increase the danger to themselves in order to lower the risk to their enemies. Nevertheless, at very least the US administration should have explained precisely why it chose not to attempt to arrest the suspects in this particular case.

There is one final doubt that can be cast on this operation: the possibility that the US might have erred in its target identification. In other words, how do we know that the people in the car were actually the people the US said they were? Because the car suffered a secondary explosion there were very few human remains and so it has proven impossible to identify the bodies positively through DNA. This has led one critic to argue that we therefore cannot be sure that the intended target – Harethi – was even in the car.[80] This is, it should be said, a largely hypothetical issue because there has been no serious suggestion that Harethi was not, in fact, killed. However, I noted earlier that one of the problems connected with an expanded right of pre-emption was an increased risk of error. In such cases, intelligence agencies should release as much information to the public as is possible and be subject to judicial oversight. Such oversight could be conducted behind closed doors in order to protect sensitive information, but it is important that states make their case as clearly and comprehensively as possible.

On balance, although significant doubts remain about whether the use of force was the only reasonable way of removing the terrorist threat and the hypothetical question of whether the right people were targeted, the Yemen missile strike can be considered a (barely) legitimate act of pre-emptive self-defence. It is important, however, that we do not simply ignore these concerns and that governments are held to account, for at least two reasons. Governments, even liberal democratic ones, can and do provide misleading information, sometimes unintentionally but sometimes deliberately. Going to war on the basis of misperceptions about an imminent threat caused by intelligence failures and/or a lack of due care is immoral, illegal and highly imprudent. The more that governments take non-governmental actors into their confidence, the more likely it is that unintentional mistakes will be exposed. The Yemen attack was the thin end of the wedge. The US did not provide the necessary evidence and information, but on the balance of probabilities its missile attack in Yemen can be viewed as just about justifiable. However, the same cannot be said of the 2003 invasion of Iraq.

Iraq

Adopting the same strategy used over Yemen, the US used three arguments to justify its decision to invade Iraq and remove Saddam Hussein's regime from power in 2003, believing that taken together three relatively unconvincing arguments amounted to a single plausible justification. The formal legal case rested on the argument that Iraq's persistent breach of Security Council 687, which had brought the 1991 Gulf War to an end, and in particular its illicit WMD programmes, invalidated the ceasefire. These ceasefire violations revived Resolution 678 authorizing use of force to remove Iraqi forces from Kuwait and restore 'regional peace and security'.[81] The UK also insisted that there was a humanitarian imperative for removing Saddam's regime, which was one of the world's worst human rights abusers. Finally, the US made a self-defence argument. In the aftermath of the war, as it became clear that Iraq, despite all its many other sins, did not in fact possess WMD or even WMD programmes, the US administration increasingly relied on the argument that the war was justified because it had made America more secure.[82] According to the Bush administration, Iraq under Saddam posed a potential if not actual threat to the US because of the potential for it to pass future WMDs to terrorists and its ability to provide a safe harbour for them.

During the protracted Security Council debate prior to the invasion, the US Ambassador John Negroponte insisted that, 'if the Security Council fails to act decisively in the event of further Iraqi violations, this resolution does not constrain any member state from acting to defend itself against the threat posed by Iraq'.[83] Ambassador Negroponte's reference to 'self-defence' clearly alluded to the US doctrine of pre-emption discussed earlier. Indeed, the idea that a right of pre-emptive self-defence might be used to legitimize an invasion of Iraq had been floated as early as June 2002. At that time, senior Defense Department officials were quoted as saying that 'Iraq has given the United States every reason under the UN Charter, which allows pre-emptive action by nations facing an imminent threat, which Saddam clearly does'.[84] Speaking shortly after the war, Bush told an ABC journalist that 'I made my decision [to go to war] based upon enough intelligence to tell me this country was threatened with Saddam Hussein in power ...' and he continued, 'America is a safer country'.[85]

Did the US satisfy the imminence and necessity tests required to justify the invasion of Iraq as an act of pre-emptive self-defence? The first question we need to consider is which standard of pre-emption should apply. The US clearly believed it should be the expanded standard intimated by the *National Security Strategy* because Iraq posed an indirect terrorist threat through its desire to acquire WMD and its links to Al Qaeda. Immediately after 11 September, Paul Wolfowitz – the neoconservative former Deputy Secretary for Defense – argued that there was between a 10 and 50 per cent chance that Iraq was involved in the terrorist attacks.[86] The administration then persistently claimed that there was 'some' link between Iraq and September 11 or, at the very least, a link between Iraq and Al Qaeda. In autumn 2002 Bush himself outlined what he believed to be the nature of the links between Iraq and Al Qaeda:

> We know that Iraq and the Al Qaeda terrorist network share a common enemy – the United States of America. We know that Iraq and Al Qaeda have had high level contacts that go back a decade. Some Al Qaeda leaders who fled Afghanistan went to Iraq ... We've learned that Iraq trained Al Qaeda members in bomb-making and poisons and deadly gases. And we know that after September the 11th Saddam Hussein's regime gleefully celebrated the terrorist attacks on America.[87]

By this logic, Iraq could decide at a moment's notice to provide Al Qaeda with chemical or biological weapons to use against the US.[88] On 5 February 2003, Colin Powell presented this case in detail to the Security Council, insisting that there was evidence of links between Iraq and Al Qaeda. He argued that since 1996, the Iraqi regime had expressed an interest in supporting Al Qaeda, had developed illicit WMD production programmes and had sought to develop a nuclear programme by purchasing uranium from Niger and that, for these reasons, it constituted a direct threat to American security.[89] He concluded that the only way to meet the danger that potential Iraqi WMD could find their way into Al Qaeda's hands was to endorse the use of force since 'the United States will not and cannot run that risk to the American people'.[90]

Empirically, this argument was always fundamentally flawed. There was only very tenuous evidence of any links between Iraq and Al Qaeda and no evidence that those links, if they existed, amounted to a cooperative relationship.[91] Indeed, there are good reasons to suggest that even American intelligence agencies believed there was nothing in the claim that Iraq and Al Qaeda cooperated with one another. The closest the US got to evidence was a memo leaked by Under Secretary of Defense, Doug Feith, that purported to contain intelligence data demonstrating cooperation between Al Qaeda and Iraq. In fact, the data simply showed that Iraqi officials had occasionally met Al Qaeda operatives. Worse, some of the intelligence reports even suggested that Iraq and Al Qaeda had actually failed to reach an understanding. As such, the Pentagon swiftly announced that the memo did not constitute evidence of a link between Iraq and Al Qaeda. As for the fact that officials from the Iraqi government had held meetings with Al Qaeda operatives, Richard Clarke – the former US counter-terrorism chief – argues that it would have been surprising had Iraqi officials *not* met Al Qaeda officials at some point. Nor, for that matter, would it have been surprising had British, American, Israeli, Iranian and other intelligence officers met with Al Qaeda operatives.[92] The fact of meetings was not enough to indicate a collaborative relationship and it is clear now that America's intelligence agencies never argued that it did.

This assessment was confirmed by the Butler Committee report on British intelligence and Iraq. Butler concluded that prior to the war, British intelligence was advising government that although there had been contact between the Iraqi regime and Al Qaeda, 'there was no evidence of cooperation'.[93] After the collapse of the Taliban in Afghanistan, Afghan refugees had established a terrorist training camp in northern Iraq, but that was in Kurdish-controlled territory, which had been placed beyond the reach of Saddam's forces partly by the no-fly zones maintained throughout the 1990s and beyond by the US and UK.[94] In September 2003, Dick Cheney was forced to admit that there was no link between Iraq and September 11, and in 2004 the administration finally admitted – though only under duress – that there probably was no cooperative relationship between Iraq and Al Qaeda either. We now know that the administration knew this to be the case in 2002–03, while it was publicly arguing to the contrary.

We can draw two conclusions from this. First, we can reject the claim that the expanded right of pre-emptive self-defence should be applied in the Iraq case. The US failed to demonstrate that an imminent terrorist threat emanated from either Iraq itself or from Iraq's alleged relationship with Al Qaeda. There were simply no reasonable grounds for believing that Iraq would pass weapons – let alone WMD – on to Al Qaeda. Second, more worryingly and contrary to the Bush administration's claims, there is little evidence to suggest that US intelligence agencies ever advised that Iraq and Al Qaeda enjoyed a cooperative relationship that might constitute a threat. According to the Butler report, the British Joint Intelligence Committee had concluded as early as late 2001 that there was no practical cooperation between Iraq and Al Qaeda. Indeed, the prospect of Iraq training and equipping Al Qaeda in chemical weaponry – directly referred to by Bush in the lead-up to the war – was not even alluded to in Britain's Joint Intelligence Committee reports.[95] As such, it seems clear that the claim of a cooperative link between Iraq and Al Qaeda was disingenuous.

There could still, however, be a case for justifying the invasion of Iraq in terms of pre-emptive self-defence if it could be demonstrated that Iraq itself posed an imminent threat. That is certainly what the UK attempted to do before the war when it released an 'intelligence dossier' that, among other things, claimed that Iraq was capable of launching a chemical or biological attack 'within forty-five minutes' – an unsubstantiated claim from a single source that was not corroborated by British intelligence.[96] The basic claim that Iraq posed an imminent threat also played a major part in Colin Powell's attempt to persuade the Security Council of the case for war. Powell argued that Iraq was deliberately concealing its WMD and missile technologies in violation of its obligations under Security

Council Resolutions 687 and 1441. He presented a series of detailed examples, which he claimed proved that Iraq had an active WMD programme. For instance, he argued that Iraq had 'mobile chemical weapons factories' and, as mentioned earlier, he claimed that Iraq had attempted to acquire nuclear material from Niger illicitly.[97] None of these claims was well founded and, in fact, all turned out to be false. The 'mobile weapons factories' turned out to be crop spraying equipment and the US State Department had demonstrated the Niger story to be a hoax even before Powell repeated it at the UN. But even if those claims could have been sustained, it would not have been enough to justify war in terms of pre-emptive self-defence. The US would still have needed to demonstrate that, in early 2003, Iraq intended to use its weapons to attack another country and that the use of force was the only reasonable way in which this threat could be removed. In the event, of course, it failed to demonstrate either of these things.

Since the invasion, it has become evident that almost all of Powell's claims were inaccurate. The Iraq Survey Group, created by the US government to investigate the state of Iraq's WMD, not only failed to find WMD but also failed to find evidence of an active WMD programme. It concluded that Iraq had no missiles capable of delivering nuclear, chemical or biological weapons, that it had unilaterally destroyed its undeclared chemical stockpiles in 1991 and had abandoned its biological warfare programme in 1995. The report also found that Iraq's former WMD programme was primarily directed at Iran and, although Saddam retained an intention to develop WMD, this goal was secondary to the goal of lifting the UN sanctions. Thus, at the time of the 2003 invasion, Iraq had neither stockpiles, nor delivery systems, nor weapons programmes and it had not had any WMD programmes for seven years.[98]

Is Iraq a case of misperception in which states misjudged the evidence and believed themselves to be threatened? On reflection, this is the most generous interpretation of the self-defence argument. As I noted earlier, there is little evidence that American or British intelligence agencies were insisting that Iraq and Al Qaeda had a cooperative relationship or that Iraq posed a specific threat. More worryingly, there is considerable evidence to suggest that the

US did not take due care in reaching its decision that Iraq posed a threat. Indeed, even prior to the war and the reports by the Iraq Survey Group and Butler Committee, there were good grounds for thinking that Iraq did not pose a threat. As well as the intelligence reports discussed above, Hans Blix, the UN's chief weapons inspector in Iraq, also insisted prior to the war that Iraq did not pose an immediate threat. On 10 February 2003, he presented a report to the Security Council which described a heightened level of Iraqi cooperation with the inspections and openly contradicted some of Powell's earlier claims about Iraq's WMD capabilities.[99] In particular, Blix argued that although the Iraqi government had still not provided full disclosure, the UN weapons inspectors had failed to find any evidence of either Iraqi WMD or an ongoing WMD programme. Meanwhile, France and Germany presented an alternative proposal for strengthening the inspections regime. Powell rejected the proposal, insisting that continued inspections would not bring about disarmament.[100] However, the increasingly positive tone of Blix's reports and the existence of a seemingly viable alternative path to disarmament made America's arguments appear increasingly incredible.

Given all this, it seems clear that in 2003 Iraq did not satisfy any of the conditions necessary to justify pre-emptive self-defence. Iraq did not pose an imminent threat in any sense of the term and given the balance of evidence, even accepting imperfect knowledge, there were not many reasonable grounds at the time for believing that it posed a threat. Moreover, as realists have argued, the use of force was not necessary because other viable and less costly courses of action remained.[101]

Conclusion

The problem with stretching an expanded right of pre-emptive self-defence is that it risks undermining the right – and more besides. Today, pre-emption is associated with Iraq and the global goodwill that emerged after 9/11. As indicated in Chapter 1, this will make it harder for the US and its allies to combat Al Qaeda. This has both moral and prudential ramifications. If, as a result of abuses such as Iraq, states and people choose to reject the idea of an expanded right of pre-emption in response to the threat of terrorism, pre-emptive attacks against terrorists are more likely to be seen as unjust. In turn, the political and material costs associated with such actions will increase, making it harder, not easier, to win the war on Al Qaeda.

FIVE

May we torture ticking-bomb terrorists?

Torture has become a fairly routine form of interrogation in the war on terror. One of the most notorious cases in North America was that of Maher Arar. On 26 September 2002 Arar, a Syrian-born Canadian engineer, was changing aircraft in New York as he returned home from holiday in Tunisia. He was detained because, it later transpired, he had been photographed drinking coffee with a suspected terrorist. He was held for thirteen days without charge in the US. Arar denied having any connection with terrorism and US authorities were unable to establish a connection. He was then placed in leg irons, taken to an executive jet and flown to Syria via Italy and Jordan. For twelve months, Arar was subjected to torture. His hands were repeatedly whipped, he was regularly beaten and was kept in a dark, damp cell. Arar was released in October 2003, after a much belated diplomatic intervention by Canada. The Syrian Ambassador in Washington announced that Syria had been unable to find any link between Arar and terrorism.[1]

Torture has also become part and parcel of American operations in Iraq. The crimes committed at Abu Ghraib are only the best known. In October 2003, coalition forces in Iraq captured the head of Iraqi air defence, General Abed Hamed Mowhoush. He died in custody on 26 November at an unnamed detention centre. The Pentagon released a death certificate declaring that Mowhoush had died of 'natural causes'. Unsatisfied with this explanation, the *Denver Post* pursued the case and forced the Pentagon to admit that an autopsy report had found that Mowhoush died of 'asphyxia due to smothering and chest compression' compounded by 'evidence of blunt force trauma to the chest and legs'.[2]

At the notorious Guantánamo Bay prison, British citizen Martin Mubanga was subjected to sensory deprivation, forced into 'stress positions', and racially and sexually abused. Ironically, Mubanga was subjected to the worst treatment at the very time that it was becoming clear to British and American officials that he had no connections whatsoever to terrorism. He was reportedly subjected to harsher treatment because Australian prisoner David Hicks, who also claimed to have been subjected to torture, had incriminated him.[3] Hicks himself later pleaded guilty to a minor charge to secure his release from Guantánamo. After holding him for five years, the US authorities failed to show that Hicks had ever actively participated in the fighting in Afghanistan or provided material support to the Taliban or Al Qaeda.

These are three of many cases of torture reported in the Western media. According to the US Defense Department, however, such acts are strictly prohibited. Detainees must be treated humanely at all times and 'there is no military necessity exception' to this rule.[4] What is more, despite the mountain of evidence to the contrary, Admiral Albert T. Church III, in his report on the Defense Department, found that there was no evidence that abuse was either officially sanctioned or caused by the placing of unreasonably high demands for information on interrogators.[5]

Admiral Church's findings were problematic in at least four respects. First, by the author's own admission, the CIA did not cooperate with the commission of enquiry. Thus, the report comments on neither the interrogation of prisoners in military camps by CIA officers nor the practice of 'extraordinary rendition' to which Arar, among others, was subjected.[6] Second, the report refers to the approval of so-called 'Category III' methods of interrogation that reportedly included 'mild, non-injurious physical contact'. Defense Secretary Donald Rumsfeld approved twenty-four interrogation techniques (out of thirty-five proposed) for use at Guantánamo Bay, aimed at 'significantly increasing the fear level in a detainee' and 'attacking or insulting the ego of a detainee'.[7] The report noted that the Chairman of the Joint Chiefs of Staff, Richard Myers, expressed doubt about their legality.[8] However, in its unclassified form the report did not specify precisely what measures were authorized. Third, the report limited itself to proven cases of abuse and did not investigate as yet unproven allegations. In the absence of external monitoring, accusations of torture are notoriously difficult to prove owing to the lack of witnesses, the use of techniques (such as near-drowning and beating the soles of the feet) designed not to leave lasting damage, and the time delay between acts of torture being committed and the victim being in a position to complain safely about them.[9] Finally, taking on board unproven allegations, there is a significant amount of circumstantial evidence to suggest that the use of torture by the US and some of its allies in the war on terror is both widespread and systematic.

Taking the three cases of torture described at the start of the chapter as examples, the geographic distance between them, the involvement of many different agencies and the similarity of the processes and techniques used point towards a coordinated strategy of information gathering based on torture. Indeed, when the US military police investigated claims of abuse at Baghdad's now notorious Abu Ghraib prison, it found that the '*systematic* and illegal abuse of detainees was intentionally perpetrated by several members of the military police guard force'.[10] Furthermore, it concluded that military intelligence officers, CIA officers and private contractors had 'actively requested that MP guards set physical and mental conditions for favourable interrogation of witnesses'.[11] There is no reason to think that the same is not true of other installations that house prisoners.

Above all, however, evidence that the use of torture in the war on terror is systematic can be gleaned from the quite open way in which successive Attorneys General attempted to create a permissive legal environment for the use of torture. John Ashcroft (2001–05) lambasted human rights activists who complained about the mistreatment of prisoners. He warned, 'to those who scare peace-loving people with phantoms of lost liberty; my message is this: Your tactics only aid terrorists'.[12] His successor Alberto Gonzales (2005–07) played a key role as White House legal counsel in sidelining the State Department's concerns about the use of torture. In a now infamous memorandum to the President on 25 January 2002, Gonzales argued that:

[T]he nature of the new war [on terrorism] places a high premium on other factors, such as the ability to quickly obtain information from captured terrorists and their sponsors in order to avoid further atrocities against American civilians ... This new paradigm renders obsolete Geneva's [the 1949 Geneva Protocol on the Treatment of Prisoners of War] strict limitations on questioning of enemy prisoners.[13]

Taken together, all of this clearly suggests that the three cases of alleged torture described earlier were not exceptions, but were part of a systematic programme designed to extract information from terrorist suspects, their associates, allies and other enemies of the US. Clearly a strategy of torture is deeply counter-productive to the war on terror. It creates martyrs, makes it easier to portray the West as barbarous and valueless, encourages Muslims to associate with extremists and against the Westerners and so-called liberals who torture them and makes it much harder to drive a wedge between the terrorists and their constituents. More directly, the imprisonment and torture of innocent people is a major propaganda coup for Al Qaeda that undoubtedly helps them to recruit young people angered by the clear injustices committed in the name of the war on terror.

The purpose of this chapter is to examine the morality of torture in a little more detail. It asks whether such a strategy is ever justifiable and whether it might be permissible to torture terrorism suspects as a rare exception when doing so is thought necessary to protect innocent lives. The argument is a little more complex than we might expect. I argue that the prohibition on torture is absolute and should be maintained but that in exceptional circumstances *desperate necessity* may dictate, though not excuse, its use – though none of the instances of torture related to the war on terror comes anywhere near this desperate necessity. This position was eloquently summarized by Slavoj Žižek, who maintained that:

[W]e can well imagine that in a specific situation, confronted with the proverbial 'prisoner who knows' and whose words can save thousands, we would resort to torture, but it is absolutely crucial that we do not elevate this desperate choice into a universal principle: following the unavoidable brutal urgency of the moment, we should simply do it. Only in this way, in the very inability or prohibition to elevate what we had to do into a universal principle, do we retain the sense of guilt, the awareness of the inadmissibility of what we had done.[14]

The first part of the chapter maps out the terrain of the debate – first demonstrating the broad consensus on the moral and legal prohibition of torture before moving on to consider, and dismiss, various attempts to justify the practice.

The legal and moral prohibition

Torture is expressly prohibited in an extensive range of human rights conventions and is widely considered a 'crime against humanity'.[15] Almost all the world's states are party to one or more conventions forbidding torture.[16] The legal prohibition of torture is widely understood as a peremptory rule, as derogation is considered impermissible. The International Covenant on Civil and Political Rights insists that no derogation from the prohibition on torture is possible even in times of 'public emergency which threatens the life of the nation' (Article 4). Both the European and American Conventions on Human Rights prohibit derogation even in times of war and public emergency, and even when those emergencies threaten the survival of the state (common Article 15). Thus the International Committee of the Red Cross has concluded that 'no possible loophole is left; there can be no excuse, no attenuating circumstances' in which torture may be permitted.[17]

The key legal question in relation to torture is therefore not so much whether it is legal, but whether specific acts that stop short of causing life-threatening pain, such as sensory deprivation, water boarding and placing people in so-called 'stress positions', are properly defined as torture. Article 1 of the UN Convention on the Prohibition of Torture and Cruel and Degrading Treatment defines torture as:

> Any act by which severe pain or suffering, whether physical or mental, is intentionally inflicted on a person for such purposes as obtaining from him or a third person information or a confession, punishing him for an act he or a third person has committed or is suspected of having committed, or intimidating him or a third

person, or for any reason based on discrimination of any kind, when such pain or suffering is inflicted by or at the instigation of or with the consent or acquiescence of a public official or other person acting in an official capacity.

In order to justify the use of forceful interrogation techniques in the war on terror, the US Defense Department has adopted two legal strategies to get around the prohibition on torture. The first has been to argue that the President's authority to manage military operations is uninhibited by international law or that individual interrogators who use torture may not be violating the prohibition because theirs is an act of national self-defence.[18] The second has been to offer a very narrow interpretation of what counts as torture. A Defense Department memorandum leaked to the media concluded that the administration of drugs to detainees would violate the prohibition of torture only if said administration was calculated to produce 'an extreme effect'.[19] Similarly, a Justice Department memorandum written by the Assistant Attorney General Jay Bybee insisted that to count as torture, a prisoner's treatment must inflict more than just moderate or fleeting pain. According to Bybee, 'torture must be equivalent in intensity to the pain accompanying serious physical injury, such as organ failure, impairment of bodily function, or even death'.[20]

The US is not the first Western state to insist that its coercive interrogation techniques are legitimate because they fall short of torture. Before the UN Convention came into force, both France and the UK made similar claims. In both cases, however, judicial authorities either rejected the claim or found that the use of measures deemed 'short of torture' were nevertheless prohibited because they were 'degrading and inhumane'. In the 1950s, French forces combating the nationalists in Algeria used torture as a standard part of its interrogation process.[21] In 1955, the government reacted to public outcries in France about the use of torture and commissioned Roger Wuillaume to conduct an investigation. The Wuillaume report called for the 'veil of hypocrisy' to be lifted and for the authorization of 'safe and controlled' coercive interrogation techniques. Permissible methods could include the use of electric shocks and the so-called 'water technique/water boarding' – holding the victim's head under water until he/she nearly drowns. According to Wuillaume such techniques were 'not quite torture'. He found that 'the water and electricity methods, provided they are carefully used, are said to produce a shock which is more psychological than physical and therefore do not constitute excessive cruelty'.[22] Nevertheless, in 2002 one of the key perpetrators and advocates of torture in Algeria, Paul Aussaresses, was found guilty of being an 'apologist for war crimes'. While his punishment was minor (a mere €7,500 fine), the judgment was crucial because the Court in effect rejected Wuillaume's argument and found that the interrogation techniques used by the French in Algeria constituted 'war crimes'.[23]

In 1971, the Compton Committee was established to investigate claims that British authorities in Northern Ireland had tortured and abused suspected IRA terrorists.[24] The committee investigated allegations relating to forty prisoners who were subjected to one or more of five methods of treatment: (1) heads covered with a black hood except when interrogated alone; (2) continual monotonous noise; (3) sleep deprivation; (4) diet of bread and water; (5) forced stress positions.[25] Much like the Wuillaume report, the Compton Committee concluded that although the five techniques constituted 'ill-treatment' they did not equate to 'physical brutality' because the interrogators did not take pleasure from inflicting pain and ill-treatment was used only for the purpose of extracting information. Because of widespread disappointment with these findings, a second enquiry was established.

The ensuing 'Parker report' went even further than Compton and defended the five techniques on the grounds that they were not excessive, that IRA terrorism had created a public emergency, and that the techniques produced valuable intelligence and saved innocent lives.[26] The Republic of Ireland took up the case in the European Commission on Human Rights. The Commission explored three illustrative cases and found that although, individually, each of the techniques did not constitute torture or degrading treatment, taken together they amounted to 'a modern system of torture falling into the same category as those systems which had been applied in previous times as a means of obtaining information and confessions'.[27]

The European Court of Human Rights overturned the decision on technical grounds but in 1979 the UK gave in to pressure and forbade use of the techniques.[28]

In both the French and British cases, the claim that certain techniques were permissible because they did not constitute torture was rejected either on the grounds that they *were* torture or that regardless of whether or not they were, they constituted 'cruel and degrading' treatment, which was also forbidden. The point here is that the contemporary American claim that certain acts designed to cause physical and/or mental pain for the purpose of extracting information does not constitute torture has been articulated before and has been found wanting.

Not only is torture considered legally wrong, there is also a broad consensus (though not unanimity) that it is morally wrong. As David Sussman put it, since the Enlightenment at least:

> [t]here has been a broad and confident consensus that torture is uniquely 'barbaric' and 'inhuman': the most profound violation possible of the dignity of a human being. In philosophical and political discussions, torture is commonly offered as one of the few unproblematic examples of a type of act that is morally impermissible without exception or qualification.[29]

But what is it about torture as opposed to simply killing someone in war that makes it so wrong? There are at least four ways of answering this question.

First, Sussman argues that torture is uniquely wrong because its ultimate goal is to force its victim into colluding against himself. The victim thus simultaneously experiences powerlessness yet is forced to be 'actively complicit in his own violation'.[30] This is wrong, Sussman argues, because it not only violates its victim's agency and autonomy, it seeks actively to pervert it.[31]

The second type of moral argument against torture is that it involves the use of violence against defenceless people and therefore violates the principle of non-combatant immunity.[32] In principle, as Henry Shue argues, torture could be justified in precisely the same way as other forms of political violence. Commonly this involves one of two approaches.

The first, popular among secular theorists, is the individual self-defence analogy: an individual is entitled to defend herself from unjust attack, even to the point of killing her assailant, so long as the killing is necessary and proportionate. Extrapolated upwards, political communities – which are amalgams of individuals – logically enjoy a collective right of self-defence.

Second, one of the basic ideas of the just war tradition is that killing is justified for the common good so long as it is conducted with right intentions. That is, the killer must be motivated by a desire to preserve peace and justice, not out of feelings of hatred or envy. According to Shue, these types of argument could be used to justify torture in cases where the victim holds information that could save civilian lives.

There is, however, one critical difference between torture and killing in the two circumstances identified above: unlike a soldier on a battlefield, the victim of torture does not pose a threat to the torturer. In other words, once someone is captured they cease to be a combatant and become a non-combatant and therefore inviolable.

Of course, this raises the issue of the 'ticking-bomb' terrorist. In those cases, where a bomb has been planted and the interrogator believes that the terrorist knows its location but is refusing to divulge that information, the terrorist cannot be properly considered a non-combatant.[33] This is a dangerous idea, however, because it could logically be expanded to cover soldiers taken captive during ongoing operations. As the soldier would undoubtedly have knowledge about the military operation that could save lives, he could plausibly be labelled a combatant for the duration of the operation and tortured. Given that we would find it intolerable to grant our enemies a right to torture our soldiers to extract information about military operations, this argument is not available to us in relation to terrorists.

The third type of moral argument is deontological (see Chapter 1). This position holds that torture is wrong because it violates fundamental principles of humanity. For some, torture is an affront to the most basic of human rights that derive from a person's very humanity. As Joel Feinberg put it:

[T]here is … no objection in principle to the idea of human rights that are absolute in the sense of being categorically exceptionless. The most plausible candidates, like the right not to be tortured, will be passive negative rights, that is, rights not to be done to by others in certain ways.[34]

The fourth type is a 'rule-utilitarian' argument that emphasizes the role of reciprocity and importance of moral consistency. Rule-utilitarians argue that the greatest good is achieved by observing a rule prohibiting torture. There are at least two good reasons to suppose this. First, the historical record demonstrates that torture is used for pernicious reasons far more often than not. It is most frequently used to silence government opponents. The prohibition of torture is therefore central for the preservation of democracy and liberal government. Second, the principle of reciprocity means that we all benefit from a rule prohibiting others from potentially torturing us at some time in the future. To reiterate a point made earlier, if an enemy can be tortured to provide life-saving information, then surely we must admit that our own soldiers, if captured, could also be tortured in order to save the lives of our enemies. Rule-utilitarians argue that the greatest good is achieved by maintaining the general prohibition on torture.[35]

There is therefore a clear consensus between international law and common morality that torture and other forms of cruel and degrading treatment against prisoners is wrong. Although loopholes may be found in individual treaties, customs or philosophical arguments, taken together they constitute a powerful case. That this is so is reflected in the fact that very few political leaders are willing publicly to defend the use of torture – a feature all too evident of the war on terror. Unfortunately, torture is a moral anomaly in that, while few if any are prepared to defend it publicly, many states either use it as a matter of course in their criminal investigations or are prepared to use it in emergencies. This creates the moral paradox whereby, on the one hand, the US and some of its allies are evidently engaged in the systematic and widespread use of torture, but on the other hand are unwilling to defend themselves publicly and have even gone on record condemning the use of torture in states such as Syria and Egypt to which they have, nevertheless, 'rendered' terror suspects.

The case for torture

Since 9/11, popular discourse, particularly in the US, has become suffused with the idea that despite the legal and moral prohibitions described in the previous section, torturing terrorists is a legitimate means of extracting information vital for the protection of US citizens. Popular television programmes 24 and *Alias* often showed terror suspects being tortured by the 'heroes'. *Alias* depicted a CIA officer suffocating a terror suspect to death. Once 'off-limits', torture is thus now widely discussed and often considered legitimate in popular discourse.[36]

These ideas have also permeated political discourse in the US. Commenting on the arrest of a senior Al Qaeda figure in late 2002, Senator Jay Rockefeller (Democrat, West Virginia), chair of the Senate Select Committee on Intelligence, told CNN that 'I wouldn't take anything off the table where he is concerned because this is a man who has killed hundreds and hundreds of Americans over the last ten years.'[37] One anonymous Defense official told the *Washington Post* 'if you don't violate someone's human rights some of the time, you probably aren't doing your job'.[38] Another unnamed official told *Newsday* that in the case of one suspect rendered from Guantánamo to Egypt 'they promptly tore his fingernails out and he started telling things'.[39] One circuit judge went as far as to insist that 'if the stakes are high enough, torture is permissible. No one who doubts that this is the case should be in a position of responsibility.'[40] Thus, when the prominent lawyer Alan Dershowitz put forth a sustained case for using legalized torture – issuing 'torture warrants' – his ideas reflected a widespread and popular sentiment.

It is important to note that the case for licensing torture put forward by Dershowitz is far from novel. His reasoning draws directly from the utilitarian defence of torture put forth by the nineteenth-century British liberal, Jeremy Bentham. Dershowitz's proposal for judicially approved 'torture warrants' drew upon the findings of Israel's 1987 Landau Commission.[41] Likewise, even prior to the Algerian war, some writers in France had also called for licensed torture.[42]

The most common defence of torture rests on act-utilitarianism (the view that an act is right or wrong, depending on its consequences) and holds that torture is permissible when cost–benefit analysis reveals that more lives are likely to be saved by resorting to torture than by choosing not to do so.[43] To satisfy Bentham, a potential torturer must pass two tests. First, it must be clear that the *purpose* behind the mistreatment of prisoners is the acquisition of information likely to save civilians. As Bentham put it:

> [f]or the purpose of rescuing from torture these hundred innocents, should any scruple be made of applying equal or superior torture, to extract the requisite information from the mouth of one criminal, who having it in his power to make known the place where at this time the enormity was practising or about the be practised, should refuse to do so?[44]

Bentham clearly believed that in such cases the greater public good required that the prisoner be tortured. The second requirement was that the torturer must be certain the victim has the information needed to save lives. No benefit is accrued by torturing those who do not have the requisite information. In short, for Bentham the torture of one guilty person for the purpose of saving more than one innocent person satisfies the cost–benefit ratio and is therefore justifiable.

The problem with Bentham's act-utilitarianism, even for those sympathetic to his case vis-à-vis torture, is the lack of guidelines for making these cost–benefit judgements. How many civilians need to be at risk to make torturing a suspect permissible? Simple cost–benefit analysis would put that figure at one or more, making torture permissible in a large number of cases. What level of proof is required that the victim holds the knowledge necessary to save lives? How does an authority employing the Benthamite system avoid the slippery slope that 'once torture is permitted on grounds of necessity, nothing can stop it from being used on grounds of expediency'?[45] To overcome these problems, Dershowitz included important safeguards in his case for legalizing torture.

The role and nature of Dershowitz's safeguards derive almost entirely from the findings of the Landau Commission. The Commission accepted the argument that Israel confronted an ongoing emergency caused by Palestinian terrorism.[46] From this, it concluded that the acquisition of information was vital to the defence of Israel and that such information was difficult to obtain. Moreover, the Commission accepted without further study the security services' claim that the use of aggressive measures was an effective means of extracting vital information. On several occasions it praised them, noting that they prevented '80–90 per cent of terrorist' attacks and that 'the overwhelming majority of those [suspected terrorists] tried were convicted on the basis of their confession alone' and accepted the security services' view that 'effective interrogation of terrorist suspects is impossible without the use of means of pressure'.[47]

All this, the Commission found, created an intolerable dilemma for the security services. Charged with the task of protecting Israelis from terrorism and confronted with the fact that the only means of extracting the necessary information was legally prohibited, security personnel were forced into committing acts they would later have to lie about. The Commission presented three options for addressing this dilemma: first, retain the status quo and leave certain interrogation techniques 'outside the realm of the law';[48] second, turn a blind eye to the use of torture – the hypocrite's position.[49] The Commission rejected both these positions on the grounds that they were legally dishonest and did not resolve the moral dilemma confronting the security services.

The third, and preferred, option, it described as 'the truthful road' and involved creating legal paths to permit torture.[50] This involved legalizing the methods already used by the security services, which were not publicized because it was argued that publication of torture methods would allow enemies to train in counter-measures, making the techniques ineffective.[51]

The system of legalized torture the Commission developed was predicated on the 'lesser evil' doctrine, a modified utilitarianism which holds that in emergencies leaders might act in immoral ways in order to protect the greater good.[52] The Commission's proposal thus contained a 'lesser evil' justification for when torture could be employed and restrictions on the types of torture that could be used in order to guard against the worst abuses.

When may torture be used? The Landau Commission's answer

to this question was predicated on the hypothetical 'ticking-bomb' terrorist. The scenario, oft-repeated, is as follows: a bomb has been planted that is likely to kill large numbers of non-combatants (in the television series 24, the bomb was nuclear). At the same time, the security services have apprehended a suspect who it believes knows the whereabouts of the bomb but is refusing to talk. It is worth quoting the Commission at length on this point, as it is pivotal to both its, and Dershowitz's, case:

> The deciding factor is not the element of time, but the comparison between the gravity of the two evils – the evil of contravening the law [prohibiting torture] as opposed to the evil that will occur sooner or later … To put it bluntly, the alternative is: are we to accept the offence of assault entailed in slapping a suspect's face, or threatening him, in order to induce him to talk and reveal a cache of explosive materials meant for use in carrying out an act of mass terror against a civilian population, and thereby prevent the greater evil which is about to occur? The answer is self-evident.[53]

Of course the answer is self-evident, because the assumptions under-lying the hypothetical case prejudge the outcome – I explore this scenario in more detail below. When applying this supposed 'lesser evil' test, the Commission found that the salient fact was not the *actual* evil threatened, but the evil that the relevant actor reasonably *believes* is imminent.[54] One final point we should notice in the above statement is the slippage between the background assumptions (a bomb has been planted and may go off at any time) and the Commission's judgement (locating an arms cache is sufficient justification). Although this will be discussed in detail later, it is necessary to draw attention to the problem here. In the first scenario – the planted bomb – the tortured suspect has a measure of control over a direct threat to non-combatants that has not diminished owing to his incarceration. The extraction of information from this suspect is *necessary and sufficient* to remove the threat. In the second scenario, the extraction of information about the location of weapons caches is *expedient* but neither *necessary* nor *sufficient* to the prevention of a specific threat.

What types of torture did the Landau schema permit? As I noted earlier, the Commission did not specify which techniques might be used. However, it outlined three important limits necessary to protect the rights of the citizen and the beneficent 'image' of the state.

1 Torture must not cause grievous harm to the suspect's honour or deprive him of human dignity.
2 Torture must not be disproportionate: the seriousness of the measures should be weighed against the potential threat that the interrogator is attempting to prevent.
3 The means of torture should be carefully controlled and limited to techniques designed not to cause lasting harm.[55]

The Israeli government did not formally act on the Commission's recommendations. However, in the mid-1990s a series of suicide bomb attacks that accompanied the collapse of the Rabin–Arafat peace process prompted attempts in the Knesset to rewrite Israel's penal code to incorporate the recommendations.[56] Moreover, Evans and Morgan argue that not only is there evidence that the measures endorsed by the Landau Commission (and others) were, indeed, used by Israel's security services, their use was officially sanctioned.[57] It could be argued, therefore, that Israel informally put the Commission's findings into practice. The Landau Commission's findings are important because they form the centrepiece of most sustained defences of the use of torture in the war on terror.

Alan Dershowitz begins his case for torture by noting that 'the tragic reality is that torture sometimes works, much though many people wish it did not'.[58] To support his claim, Dershowitz points to the foiling of a 1995 plot to crash eleven commercial aircraft simultaneously over the Pacific and crash a Cessna filled with explosives into the CIA's headquarters. According to Dershowitz, the Philippines police arrested and tortured a suspect (breaking most of his ribs in the process) over sixty-seven days until he divulged the information necessary to foil the plot. It is precisely because torture sometimes works that states around the world continue to use it, he contends.

Despite his avowed intellectual debt to Bentham, Dershowitz is not an act-utilitarian. He insists that there are basic human rights and that the costs of breaching them are high. Nevertheless, political leaders have a responsibility to get 'dirty hands' and pay the costs of rule-breaking in order to save innocent lives. To balance these two sets of obligations, Dershowitz follows Bentham and the Landau Commission in predicating his case for legalized torture on the hypothetical 'ticking-bomb terrorist'. In contrast to earlier writers, however, Dershowitz expands his argument to suggest that if torture can be justified in 'ticking-bomb' cases why not in other cases where judicial authorities may issue 'torture warrants'. Similarly, Fritz Allhoff argues that the criterion should not be a ticking bomb but the prevention of future threats.[59]

The case for 'torture warrants' is based on Dershowitz's observation that in liberal societies such as the US there are not two, but three, fundamental value sets at stake: (1) the safety and security of the nation's citizens; (2) the preservation of individual human rights; (3) democratic openness and accountability. Legitimate governments simply cannot breach the first set of values (1). The just war tradition permits the use of violence – and hence the breach of human rights – against enemies in just wars. Thus, according to Dershowitz, only pacifists can complain about the violation of enemy combatants' human rights (2). Torturing an enemy combatant to acquire information that will save lives is no different from killing him in battle to accomplish the same thing. According to the just war tradition, combatants lose their right not to be attacked when they obtain their right to use force against enemy combatants.[60] Maintaining the hypocrisy of practising torture but keeping it 'off the books' by either denying its existence or placing it above the law violates both values 2 and 3. The breach of value 3 is particularly problematic for Dershowitz, because public justification and scrutiny is crucial to deciding whether particular acts should be committed. Moreover, by removing judicial oversight all three approaches outlined by the Landau Commission fail because criminals cannot be convicted if their means of interrogation cannot be disclosed and scrutinized in court.

Dershowitz therefore proposes a change in the law, to permit judicial authorities to issue 'torture warrants'. Being open about the use of torture would permit both judicial oversight and public discussion about the appropriate balance to be struck between the three sets of values. Under Dershowitz's system, law enforcement agencies would need to apply to judicial authorities for torture warrants and demonstrate what they planned to do, when, and the necessity of torture. Judges would decide the merits of the case and rule accordingly. In all cases, complete records would be kept. The system would contain restrictions on who could be tortured (Dershowitz bases his claim on the ticking-bomb case but insists that judges be free to determine each case on its merits and that satisfactory necessity arguments may also be levelled in non-ticking-bomb cases) and what methods could be used (he rules out potentially lethal measures and measures that could cause permanent physical or psychological damage). Dershowitz identifies two particular methods that cause excruciating pain without lasting damage: injecting air below the fingernails and drilling teeth without anaesthetic. This system, Dershowitz argues, would permit law enforcement agencies to use measures to extract vital life-saving information from terrorist suspects, while guarding against potential abuse. Bringing torture into the open would make it more humane and afford greater protection to its victims.

Dershowitz's case for creating a legal framework for torture is predicated on the idea that torture works, that security services will therefore inevitably use it to prevent terrorism, and that the best way to protect the victims of torture, prevent abuse and facilitate transparency is to create a framework for legalization. At face value this is an appealing argument inasmuch as it promises to create safeguards and forces liberal societies to acknowledge their own dirty hands in the fight against terrorism. However, it is dangerously flawed in at least three important respects.

The first problem is that it is predicated on the false assumption that torture works. That is, the use of torture facilitates the extraction of information from terror suspects that helps to save lives. Dershowitz's belief in the utility of torture comes from two sources: the Landau Commission's findings and a 1995 case where torture was used ostensibly to foil a massive terrorist attack over the Pacific. Interestingly, the Landau Commission did not itself investigate the utility of torture in specific cases and simply accepted the Israeli security services' insistence that torture was effective in certain circumstances.[61] On the Philippines case, Dershowitz cites a *Washington Post* report to support his case that the Philippines government tortured a suspected terrorist until he revealed details of a plot to blow up eleven aircraft simultaneously over the Pacific.[62] What is in doubt is not that the Philippines tortured a suspect nor that they uncovered a plot, but that the use of torture prevented the plot from being actualized. Other reports at the time suggest that it was the discovery of documents at the suspect's home following a fire that tipped police off. Given that it took sixty-seven days of torture to extract the information it seems highly unlikely that torture would have prevented the plot had the threat been imminent.[63] Other writers point to alternative sources to support their claim that torture works – especially the French experience in Algeria.[64]

There are at least two other reasons to doubt the claim that torture is an effective means of extracting life-saving information: there is no consensus about this even within the US security services and the purported 'success' of the use of torture by the French in Algeria is, at best, ambiguous. I will address each in turn.

The view presented in Dershowitz's argument strongly implies a consensus among security agencies about the utility of torture. In fact, there were sharp disagreements among US interrogators. One former FBI counter-terrorist interrogator was quoted as arguing that interrogating, for instance, a naked Muslim fundamentalist was difficult because 'he's going to be ashamed, and humiliated, and cold. He'll tell you anything you want to hear to get his clothes back. There's no value in it.'[65] The problems appear to be twofold. On the one hand, it is important to distinguish between confessions and live-saving intelligence. While torture is effective at extracting the former, there are doubts about its ability to do the latter. There are now numerous cases of terror suspects giving false confessions under torture. The former British Ambassador to Uzbekistan, Craig Murray, reported that the Uzbek authorities used torture (such as partial boiling) to extract information from suspected terrorists, which would then be passed on to the US and UK. Murray insisted that:

[T]his material is useless. We are selling our souls for dross. Tortured dupes are forced to sign confessions showing what the Uzbek government wants the US and UK to believe – that they and we are fighting the same war on terror.[66]

In another case, three British suspects confessed under torture to having been trained at Al Qaeda camps in Afghanistan. British intelligence, however, produced conclusive evidence that the three were actually in Britain at the time they were supposed to have been in Afghanistan.[67] As is well documented, live-saving intelligence is usually extracted in the first hours after a suspect is apprehended. Once a suspect's incarceration becomes known to the terrorist organization, the organization tends to change its plans. The longer the suspect is held, the less vital any information he could offer becomes. After a few days, the suspect is unable to offer anything useful about ongoing operations. Torture may well be a useful way of extracting confessions and incriminations but there is much less evidence to suggest that it is an effective way of extracting life-saving information.

The claim that the use of torture by the French in Algeria provides evidence of its effectiveness is also questionable.[68] General Massu, the commander of French forces in the 'battle of Algiers' who, in the 1970s, defended the widespread use of torture later disputed the claim. According to Massu in 1992, torture served no 'necessary or useful purpose' in combating terrorists in Algeria.[69] Indeed, France ultimately lost the Algerian war. This has led some scholars to argue that although torture may have delivered some short-term tactical advantages, in the longer term it had at least two consequences that worsened France's predicament.

The use of torture helped France lose the battle for hearts and minds. On the one hand, it contradicted the humanistic and civilizing mission used to justify French rule in Algeria, undermining the French claim to legitimacy there. On the other hand, it created a powerful reaction among Algerians and helped strengthen the nationalists, contributing significantly to France's ultimate defeat.[70]

The widespread use of torture contributed to the general brutalization of Algerian society by encouraging white settlers to pursue their aims through force of arms, creating martyrs among the nationalists and establishing a normative context that enabled the nationalist rebels to employ similarly brutal techniques against their enemies.[71] This is not the place to decide the utility of torture in detail. What we need to note here, however, is that its utility is contested even among those who have practised it. As such, it is doubtful whether the utility argument can carry the weight that Dershowitz and others give it.

The second problem with legalizing torture is that doing so would require changes to one of the just war tradition's most fundamental principles: non-combatant immunity. By its very nature, torture involves deliberately inflicting harm upon non-combatants. Once terror suspects are taken prisoner they cease being combatants because they no longer pose a threat. Therefore, torture is wrong for precisely the same reason as terrorism: because it involves harming non-combatants. One cannot, therefore, justify torture without opening the door to the justification of terrorism.

The third problem with legalized torture is that it cannot be consistently applied. In Chapter 1 I took a lead from Immanuel Kant in arguing that one of the key tests for any moral principle is whether it is generalizable – whether it can be applied consistently in every case. If we consider the likely effects of generalizing a right to torture, at least two deeply troubling outcomes emerge. First, the vast majority of torturers, both during the Cold War and today, use torture to silence political opponents.[72] From China and Burma, to Egypt, Syria, Sudan, North Korea, Pakistan and the Philippines, torture is used primarily as a form of regime maintenance. If states such as these – and many more besides – were given a moral right to legalize torture, there is little doubt that far from curtailing it, it would have the effect of normalizing torture, making it more widespread. The result would be much more global torture, mostly aimed at the opponents of oppressive regimes. Second, a generalizable moral principle is one that others can invoke against citizens of Western states. If all states were permitted to legalize torture in order to extract information that might save lives, the citizens of Western states could also be subjected to torture, potentially legitimately, in places such as Iran, Serbia, Afghanistan, Libya, China and North

Korea. In the changed normative context of a universal right to legalized torture, we would lose the moral language necessary to condemn the torture of our fellow citizens.

Taken together, these three arguments constitute a powerful case against the generalized legalization of torture proposed by Dershowitz and others. Their case is predicated on a simple utilitarian argument but the claim at its heart – that torturing suspected terrorists saves lives – is heavily contested, even among interrogators. It involves changing arguably the most fundamental rule of the just war tradition and endorsing acts expressly prohibited by an unusually high number of legal texts. Finally, it involves advancing a moral argument that cannot be generalized without producing deeply troubling effects. There remains, however, the question of the 'ticking-bomb' terrorist from which Dershowitz extrapolates his more generalized case.

The ticking-bomb terrorist

The argument that torture is sometimes legitimate tends to start with the 'ticking-bomb' terrorist case. This scenario was first articulated by Bentham and reappears in virtually every recent justification of torture. It is the starting point of Dershowitz's argument and the scenario presented to audiences in television programmes such as 24 and *Alias*. Despite its omnipresence in public discourse, I have uncovered only one recorded case of a ticking-bomb terrorist. In 1957, Paul Teitgen, the Secretary General of the Algiers Prefecture, was confronted with precisely this dilemma. The Chief of Police requested that Teitgen authorize the torture of Fernand Yveton, a communist insurgent caught in the act of planting a bomb at a gasworks. The Chief of Police believed that Yveton had planted a second bomb and feared that if it was detonated it would cause a gas explosion, killing potentially thousands of civilians. Teitgen refused to authorize the torture. According to his own account he 'trembled the whole afternoon. Finally the bomb did not go off. Thank God I was right. Because if you once get into this torture business, you're lost.'[73]

Despite the proposition that in the only recorded case of a ticking-bomb terrorist, torture was not authorized and no bombs exploded, it is fair to suggest that the hypothetical scenario is designed to prejudge the moral outcome. In this hypothetical case, only pacifists would deny the resort to torture. The ticking-bomb scenario relies on four conditions being satisfied: the interrogators must be sure they have the right person; they must be certain the suspect holds the information they need to avert an imminent threat and save lives; they must be sure that the use of torture will help the interrogator secure the necessary information; and the information elicited must be reliable.[74] The hypothetical case certainly highlights an instance in which lesser evil considerations may dictate breaking the prohibition on torture, but that is precisely what the assumptions are intended to do. It is worth quoting Henry Shue at length:

> I can see no way to deny the permissibility of torture in a case *just like this* ... But there is a saying in jurisprudence that hard cases make bad law, and there might well be one in philosophy that artificial cases make bad ethics. If the example is made sufficiently extraordinary, the conclusion that the torture is permissible is secure. But one cannot easily draw conclusions for ordinary cases from extraordinary ones, and as the situation described becomes more likely, the conclusion that the torture is permissible becomes more debatable.[75]

Certainly none of the alleged instances of torture that have emerged in relation to the war on terror comes close to the ticking-bomb scenario. Neither, for that matter, does the Philippines case cited by Dershowitz, even if we put aside doubts about the function of torture in that case. Given that, the use of the ticking-bomb terrorist scenario to defend a broader right to torture is moral casuistry at its worst.

Another problem with creating an exception to the ban on torture in cases of 'ticking-bomb' terrorists is slippage: in a particular campaign torture may be initially reserved for extreme and exceptional cases but as the practice becomes normalized the threshold for its use drops from the need to extract information necessary and sufficient to save lives to the desire to extract expedient information. There is circumstantial evidence that this has already happened in the 'war on terror'. Whereas at the outset torture was reserved for 'high-value' Al Qaeda figures who, it was believed, would be able to divulge Al Qaeda's future plans, the US President's authority to exercise all necessary measures has been used to cover the torture of suspects such as Maher Arar and former Australian Guantánamo detainee Mamduh Habib, who were always unlikely to have had any such information.[76]

More detailed evidence of slippage is available in the Algerian case where, as Shue argues, torture was first justified as a rare measure to prevent imminent attacks on civilians but spread 'like a cancer' until it became normal practice. 'The problem', Shue argued, 'is that torture is a shortcut, and everybody loves a shortcut.'[77] According to Vidal-Naquet's account, the practice began as a clandestine method of interrogation utilized by the police. At the beginning of the war, in 1955, the police rounded up people suspected of collaborating with the nationalists and tortured many of them. This practice spread from the police into the army and beyond until it became a 'state institution'.[78] How did this happen?

At the outset of the war, the military was overseen by a judicial process for reviewing the death of nationalists, even those killed in combat. As Soustelle recounts:

> When a *fellegh* [nationalist rebel] was killed, the Public Prosecutor immediately opened an enquiry as he would have in the case of a murder in peacetime and the examining Magistrate would compel astonished, and often indignant, officers and soldiers to appear and justify their conduct in the face of the enemy, just as if they had committed a civil crime.[79]

As the war progressed, the French military came to believe that the nationalists were indoctrinating the population at large and using a wide network of informants to keep abreast of French military movements.[80] In response, the military developed a strategy of 'protection-commitment-supervision'. In order to 'protect' the civilian population, potentially dangerous groups such as nomadic tribes were herded into camps. The 'commitment' element involved forcibly securing the collaboration of a proportion of the Muslim population in order to counter the perceived intelligence superiority enjoyed by the nationalists. The third element, 'supervision', involved the close monitoring of civilians, which in turn warranted closer cooperation between the army and the police.[81] Despite some internal opposition within the military, Algeria was gradually taken over by an autonomous military authority. In early 1957, police powers in Algiers were formally signed over to the military.

By this stage, the normative context had also changed. In the aftermath of the Wuillaume report, the judicial atmosphere became more permissive and the use of torture was widely accepted within French circles in Algeria. This was facilitated by the widespread use of the 'ticking-bomb' scenario as justification. At the time Father Delarue, an army chaplain, wrote that:

> Faced with a choice between two evils, either to cause temporary suffering to a bandit taken in the act who in any case deserves to die, or to leave numbers of innocent people to be massacred by this criminal's gang, when it could be destroyed as a result of his information, there can be no hesitation in choosing the lesser of the two evils, in an effective but not sadistic interrogation.[82]

In practice, 'protection-commitment-supervision' involved the use of torture in far more circumstances than Delarue's formulation suggested. As well as internment, 'protection' also involved torturing and killing non-combatants as a deterrent to others contemplating assisting the rebels. 'Commitment' involved using torture to extract information about the rebels' chain of command, leadership, and training methods.[83] At the outset of the infamous 'Battle of Algiers', General Massu prepared a note for distribution among the army which insisted that 'a *sine qua non* of our action in Algeria is that we should accept these [torture] methods heart and soul as necessary and morally justifiable'.[84] In other words, whereas torture was initially viewed and was still justified as an exceptional measure, it had become a core tactic in pursuit of the strategic plan. (Recall the dilemma that confronted Paul Teitgen, discussed earlier.) After police powers were assigned to the military, Teitgen was obliged to sign at least 24,000 confinement orders and by his own reckoning at least 3,024 of those people disappeared – victims of either torture or summary execution. Teitgen resigned in protest on 12 September 1957.[85]

According to Vidal-Naquet, the 'cancer' of torture spread still further – to the judiciary, giving us good grounds for scepticism about the effectiveness of Dershowitz's 'torture warrants'. On the rare occasion where members of the security services were brought before a court on charges of torture, cases were either dismissed or derisory punishments given. On one occasion, three policemen who admitted electrocuting three Algerian prisoners were given $15 fines. On another, three men who admitted torturing a Muslim woman to death were acquitted. A network of magistrates with close links to the security services was developed. Such magistrates either turned a blind eye to torture or tacitly authorized its use.[86]

The French experience in Algeria therefore provides a salient warning about the dangers of slippage and normalization. During the course of war, torture 'infected' the police, army and judiciary, first as an exceptional measure only rarely used but by 1957 as a routine part of interrogation. Paul Teitgen's experience provides a seminal example of slippage at work. At first, as I noted earlier, Teitgen refused to sanction the torture of even a ticking-bomb terrorist. By the time he resigned in September 1957, however, over 3,000 'disappearances' had occurred as a result of arrests he had sanctioned. What is more, far from Dershowitz's expectation that judicial oversight would limit and control torture, the Algerian case suggests that the partial legalisation endorsed by the Wuillaume Commission and the normative context it helped create only contributed to the institutionalization and hence spread of torture.

As I mentioned earlier, there is circumstantial evidence that slippage and normalization are occurring in the war on terror, and evidence from Israel, the UK and elsewhere suggests that in normative contexts when the judiciary is prepared to tolerate torture, its use spreads and the scale and gravity of abuse worsens. Moreover, as the Algerian case demonstrates only too well, there is a real danger that by permitting or excusing torture in the 'ticking-bomb terrorist' scenario, it becomes easier to justify torture in cases that fall just short of this scenario: we can torture suspects who may know where the arms cache is; where the plans are laid; what the training techniques were; how the rebels organize themselves. Over time, it becomes permissible to torture terrorist suspects simply because they *are* terrorist suspects.

This leaves us with the question of the ticking-bomb terrorist. What should interrogators and political leaders do when faced with this tragic choice in a situation precisely like the one set out in the scenario – however unlikely that scenario might be? Creating an exception to the prohibition on torture, or even permitting torturers to plead necessity in mitigation is dangerous because it leads to slippage. If a torturer succeeds in a mitigation argument, this has the effect of changing the moral prohibition of torture by, in effect, creating an exception to the general ban. Once the exception becomes the norm, the possibility is opened for other types of mitigation pleas that fall short of the ticking-bomb scenario. In its Northern Ireland ruling, the European Commission on Human Rights attempted to overcome this problem by drawing attention to the limits of mitigation. As the Commission put it:

> It is not difficult, to take a hypothetical situation, to imagine the extreme strain on a police officer who questions the prisoner about the location of a bomb which has been timed to explode in a public area within a very short while ... any strain on the members of the security forces cannot justify the application on a prisoner of treatment amounting to a breach of Art. 3. On the other hand, as a matter of fact, the domestic authorities are likely to take into account the general situation as a mitigating circumstance in determining the sentence or other punishment to be imposed on the individual ... for acts of ill-treatment ... However, where a penalty has been so mitigated by the domestic judicial or disciplinary authorities, having due regard for the severity of the acts involved and *the necessity of preventing their repetition,* this fact cannot in itself be regarded as tolerance on the part of these authorities.[87]

This is a sophisticated argument because it insists that not only should authorities take the extreme circumstances into consideration, they should also be guided by the *necessity* of preventing further occurrences – and slippage – in making their judgments about the legality of torture in particular cases. The desire to mitigate in the face of exceptional circumstances must be balanced against the necessity of preventing slippage.

The value of this argument is that it captures Žižek's concern that by elevating the idea of the use of torture in ticking-bomb cases to the status of a general principle we risk tacitly legitimizing torture. In cases *exactly* like this, interrogators may be forced by 'the unavoidable brutal urgency of the moment' to torture the suspect. This is a desperate and tragic choice. The sense of tragedy is captured by the Commission's insistence that not only does the utilitarian justification fail to excuse the crime, in any given case the weight of circumstance as a mitigating factor must be balanced against the requirement to prevent further violations of the law. Thus, when forced by the desperate urgency of the moment to torture a suspected ticking-bomb terrorist the interrogator cannot know the extent to which the circumstances will mitigate the punishment he/she will receive for the wrong about to be committed. Of course, in genuinely 'urgent' situations, the interrogator will not have time to make such calculations.

The Commission's findings are dependent on a number of factors not normally present in contexts where torture is being administered. This in itself provides a valuable test. The Commission assumes that all suspects have access to the law, that cases of torture will be reported, and that the judiciary exercises effective and independent oversight. By contrast, torture thrives when it is placed beyond the law: when basic rights such as *habeas corpus* are suspended; where judicial authorities and defence lawyers are unable to oversee imprisonment and interrogation; where the hierarchy of judiciary, executive and military/police authority becomes blurred. This is precisely what happened in Algeria and there are strong parallels between this and US policies such as 'extraordinary rendition', detention without trial, the denial of independent legal representation, and denial of access to regular courts.[88] It is inescapable that such measures go hand in hand with normalized torture and encourage slippage. A useful first test in evaluating a specific ticking-bomb terrorist case therefore is to ascertain the normative context in which it takes place. A reasonable balance between the exceptional circumstances and the necessity of prevention depends upon the preservation of a normative context hostile to torture. Where rights associated with detention begin to be eroded, the state concerned cannot reasonably claim to be fulfilling its moral and legal duty to prevent torture.

Beyond that, the Commission's recommendation forces the interrogator and those who authorize the use of torture to get 'dirty hands' in the fullest sense. As Walzer put it, the doctrine of 'dirty hands' insists that political and military leaders 'may sometimes find themselves in situations where they cannot avoid acting immorally'.[89] By not stipulating the considerations that may be taken into account in mitigation and by insisting that the urge to mitigate be balanced against the necessity of preventing recurrence, the Commission's formula, though crafted in legal terminology, provides a useful moral framework by introducing uncertainty. Those who torture terrorist suspects cannot know beforehand whether their actions will be tolerated. The decision of whether to commit acts of torture depends on a wider balance of factors.

How are such judgements to be made? On the one hand, there is the case in hand. To what extent did the interrogator have grounds for reasonably believing the suspect to be a ticking-bomb terrorist? The hypothetical case suggests near certainty and this seems to be a reasonable expectation. Only if there are very good reasons to believe that the suspect knows when and where the bomb will explode can he be tortured. We also need to ask about the gravity of the threat. Are non-combatants at risk? How many? Can the risk be averted in any other way (such as evacuation)? This, in a sense, is the proportionality criterion: is the threat sufficiently grave to create the desperate need to torture the suspect? These considerations need to be balanced against the *necessity* of preventing further recurrences of torture. Torturers may still be condemned, for instance, if there is a risk of precedent setting. Alternatively, if the torturer does not consider himself guilty of a grave wrong or attempts to justify the act through act-utilitarian arguments, the need to prevent may override the mitigating circumstances in shaping the moral and legal response to the case. Similarly, the individual case needs to be situated within a wider context. Is the case under scrutiny part of a pattern or is it genuinely unique? Has a normative context conducive to torture been created? Is it copying similar earlier cases? Was the interrogator trained in torture techniques?

For all the reasons outlined above, we should avoid the temptation of permitting the torture of the ticking-bomb terrorist just as much as we should avoid the temptation to rule it out in every conceivable case. Moral and legal uncertainty guards against slippage and normalization, while not prejudging the outcome of individual cases. Instead, in each case the mitigating circumstances need to be balanced against the broader necessity of preventing torture. It is important that the torturer and those who authorize torture do not know the likely moral and legal assessment of their action beforehand. Such uncertainty forces them to accept dirty hands: to realize that their own society and the wider world may regard them as immoral and criminal for what they are about to do.

Conclusion

The US and its allies have clearly prioritized the acquisition of intelligence over the moral and legal constraints on violence and there is no justification for the use of force. By doing so, they risk undermining their liberal agenda in the Middle East and elsewhere as they ally with some of the world's most notorious human rights abusers in blocking moves to combat torture. Moreover, they violate and risk undermining the prohibition of torture and, in turn, wider principles of discrimination and proportionality. That is no way to win a battle of ideas against Al Qaeda terrorists and their allies.

SIX
What comes next?

As I noted in Chapter 1, when political leaders take the decision to go to war it is morally imperative they do so with a clear end in sight. But, as I noted in Chapter 3, because a 'war on terror' is open-ended, does not specify an opponent and has an unclear objective, it is very difficult to know when the war has ended and when victory can be declared. It is therefore not surprising that commentators and strategists have been hard pressed to tell us whether we are winning the war. Should our guide be the global incidence of terrorism? If so, we are clearly losing. Should we be guided by the more modest goal of restricting Al Qaeda terrorism? Or should our benchmark fall somewhere between the two and focus on the ability of Middle Eastern extremists to export terror to the West and beyond? Without clear guidance on what the war on terror is actually trying to do, it will be almost impossible to determine whether we are winning, have won or have suffered setbacks. This inability also contributes to the basic immorality of a war on terrorism. Because we cannot specify who the enemy is and what threat they pose, we cannot begin to make a case for just cause or proportionality. The first task for political leaders and their advisers therefore is to identify precisely what the war on terror is about and from that to identify how the war might be brought to an end.

One way of doing this, proposed in Chapters 3 and 4, is to see the war on terror not as a single whole, but as a number of inter-secting military engagements, each of which needs to be justified on its own merits by reference to the moral framework set out in Chapter 1. Approaching the war on terror in this way brings us to the question of what a just peace might look like. In other words, what are we fighting for and what is the legitimate end state? This is sometimes referred to as the *jus post bellum* part of the just war tradition – justice *after* war. Because it is more recent, *jus post bellum* is much less well developed than the other elements of the tradition. Indeed, there are those – myself included – who doubt whether there is in fact a third plank in just war thinking. Whatever we think of the relative merits of *jus post bellum*, however, it cannot be denied that a moral assessment of the elements of the war on terror has to take account of the justice of the peace that will follow it. The purpose of this chapter, therefore, is to set out the parameters of that discussion and reflect on the morality of different war-endings. I begin by setting out two ways of understanding *jus post bellum* – the minimalist and maximalist approaches.

The minimalist approach

This approach holds that the main purpose of *jus post bellum* is to prevent excesses by victors through limiting what they are entitled to do. Drawing upon the quasi-judicial concept of the just war evident in the work of Grotius and Vattel as well as philosophers such as Kant (see Chapter 1), minimalists tend to argue that combatants are entitled to wage war only to the point at which their rights are vindicated.[1] Because the minimalist account of *jus post bellum* draws its authority from direct reference to particular elements of the just war tradition, it is worth briefly considering these.

According to Vattel:

> [W]hen a sovereign has been forced to go to war from just and weighty reasons, he may continue the operations of the war until he has attained the lawful object of it, which is to obtain justice and to put himself in a state of security.[2]

If the victors enforce a peace that goes beyond the legitimate vindication of rights, they potentially create grounds for a just war to be waged against them, if the other *jus ad bellum* criteria are satisfied.[3]

The conception of legitimate war as a quasi-judicial activity involving rights vindication has long been a staple of just war thinking and became prominent after the just war tradition's turn towards secularism in the sixteenth century.[4] Gentili argued that no war was just unless it was absolutely necessary and insisted that war became necessary only when every other avenue for resolving a conflict had been explored and there was no means of arbitration. A reluctance to submit to impartial arbitration, he argued, exposed a sovereign's doubts about the justice of his own case.[5] Grotius also defined just war in quasi-judicial terms. The only just cause for war, he argued, was an injury received in a context where tribunals were either ineffective or without jurisdiction. Grotius thus conceived three 'images' of just war: war as judicial act; war as litigation; and war as defence of the common good.[6] In short, justified war was a means of protecting or enforcing rights in an international anarchy where there was no possibility of authoritative arbitration.

What are these rights that states can enforce through war and where do they come from? Unsurprisingly, the writers cited above articulated subtly different lists. In the contemporary world, the rights enjoyed by states are tempered in important respects by international law – almost entirely neglected by advocates of *jus post bellum* – which insists that there are only two types of lawful war: wars of self-defence and collective enforcement authorized by the UN Security Council.

Grotius identified four just causes for war and, like some of his predecessors, rejected the legitimacy of both 'divinely commanded' war and war to enforce religious orthodoxy. Two of Grotius's just causes were grounded in natural law: the right of self-defence (grounded in the principle of self-preservation) and the right to punish wrongdoers. As I noted in Chapter 4, the right of self-defence included a limited right of pre-emption in situations where there was a clear, specific and imminent threat but, like Gentili, Grotius argued that a generalized fear of some future threat did not provide grounds for war. In cases where 'an attack by violence is made on one's person, endangering life, and no other way of escape is open, under such circumstances war is permissible, even though it involve the slaying of the assailant'.[7] This right, however, was limited to cases where the threat was 'immediate and imminent'.[8] The right to punish wrongdoers pertained only to circumstances where the wrong committed was 'unambiguously destructive' of society. The other two just causes were grounded in judicial law: the enforcement of legal rights and the reparation of injuries where no other avenue was available.

Vattel's system was predicated on the view that nations were free, independent and equal in nature. From this he drew the idea that separate nations should be considered sovereign and that such entities ought to be considered equal.[9] He understood international law as 'the science of the rights which exist between Nations or States, and of the obligations corresponding to those rights'.[10] Vattel insisted that sovereigns had an inherent right to wage war and agreed with the Grotian premise that the *jus ad bellum* was a largely procedural matter dependent on the satisfaction of the rightful authority and prior declaration criteria, though this did not entirely exonerate sovereigns from their culpability under natural law.[11] Vattel considered both defensive and offensive wars to be potentially legitimate, with the key criteria being that 'the cause of every just war is an injury either already received, or threatened'.[12] Reiterating the classic just war doctrine on just cause, Vattel argued that there were three such causes: claiming rightfully owned property, punishing the aggressor or offender, and self-defence.[13]

For proponents of a minimalist approach to *jus post bellum*, then, victors are entitled to protect themselves, recover that which was illicitly taken, punish the perpetrators and – in the Grotian but not the Vattelian schema – prevent, halt and/or punish those who gravely violate common morality by, for instance, engaging in systematic and widespread terrorism.[14] This may involve the military occupation of territory but minimalism draws a sharp distinction between occupation and the full assumption of the reins of government, particularly if the latter involves imposing a particular form of government on the vanquished. According to one interpretation of the Hague Regulations and Geneva Conventions, occupying powers are entitled to assume only the role of de facto administrators, and 'unwarranted interference in the domestic affairs of the occupied territory' is incompatible with the law of occupation.[15] The limit of what constitutes 'unwarranted interference' was set out more clearly in the 1907 Hague Regulations, which insisted that the occupying power respect the laws in force in the country 'unless absolutely prevented' from doing so (Article 43). This duty, however, was subject to the limitations and responsibilities imposed by international human rights standards.

Linking the victors' rights to the just causes for war begs the further question of whether states are entitled only to restore the status quo. Most advocates of *jus post bellum* are adamant that just belligerents are entitled to do more than simply restore the status quo. Indeed, Orend and Walzer strongly imply that they are *required* to do more. They argue that the reason is straightforward. By definition, the pre-war status quo included the seeds of future conflict. The basic just war idea – that wars are fought to preserve the peace – means that the victors are certainly entitled and possibly obliged to remove those seeds of potential future war in order to satisfy *jus post bellum* – because a peace that contains the seeds of future war cannot, by this account, be considered just.[16] The problem, as Orend sees it, is exacerbated by the fact that war itself is so destructive and changes so much that the purpose must be a more secure peace. Thus he argues that the aim of a just war must be 'a *more secure possession of our rights*, both individual and collective. The aim of the just and lawful war is the resistance of aggression and the vindication of the fundamental rights of political communities.'[17] Both Orend's and Walzer's language implies a degree of obligation that sits uncomfortably with minimalist *jus post bellum*. With that in mind, I suggest (following Vattel) that according to the minimalist version of *jus post bellum* the victor *may* continue the war 'to obtain justice and to put himself in a state of security' but is entitled to choose not to, and decide instead to settle for the restoration of the status quo.[18]

Matters are made more complex, however, because contemporary international law relating to just cause is at variance with both the Grotian and Vattelian ideas, which are to a greater or lesser extent used by advocates of the minimalist version of *jus post bellum*. The UN Charter expressly prohibits the threat or use of force in international relations (Article 2 [4]) except when used in self-defence (Article 51) or when authorized by the UN Security Council for the purpose of maintaining international peace and security (Article 39). In essence, initiating war for whatever purpose without the authorization of the UN Security Council is illegal, so states using force would have to prove that they acted either in self-defence or with the approval of the host government.

Clearly, this poses a problem for the minimalist approach because it suggests a much more limited list of rights that can be legally vindicated. Which version of rights should provide the basis for a minimalist conception of *jus post bellum?* Both just war writers and legal theorists have attempted to get around this, and similar problems associated with other aspects of the legitimacy of war, by insisting upon a radical separation of international law and the just war tradition. There are a number of problems with this. First and foremost, it does not help us ascertain whether a minimalist conception of *jus post bellum* should be predicated on the Grotian and Vattelian suites of rights or on the narrower legal rights and duties afforded to states. Without an answer to this question, it is impossible for us to know what victors are entitled to do after war. Also, in practice, individual ethical and legal arguments provide only part of the broader justifications for recourse to war and the justice of peace. Finally, separating law from the wider just war tradition does a historical disservice to the tradition by unduly narrowing its scope.

An alternative way of thinking about this problem is to follow Ian Clark, who suggested that legitimacy judgements are shaped by the balance between ethical, legal and political considerations.[19] According to this perspective, what rights may be legitimately vindicated in a particular case depends upon the appropriate balance between these considerations at any given time or place. Although some just war theorists will no doubt criticize this view because of the secondary role given to justice, for the minimalist approach to be politically and intellectually coherent it is necessary to avoid drawing up comprehensive lists of rights that may be vindicated by the peace. There is instead the basic minimalist view that the *jus post bellum* should be limited to the vindication of those rights that gave just cause for war in the first place. This does, however, open the door to the argument that minimalism makes *jus post bellum* redundant because it is based on rights and limits already covered by traditional just war thinking.

There are at least three further problems associated with the application of *jus post bellum*. The first is the place of the law of occupation in this schema. The 1949 Geneva Convention on the

Protection of Civilians (Convention IV) devoted its attention to providing a comprehensive system of protection for non-combatants in occupied territories, spending only a short time on blanket provisions for non-combatants in general.[20] It shared the minimalist interest in restraining the victors after war. As Geoffrey Best explained, the Convention's primary concern was to set limits upon what occupying forces could do to civilians in occupied territories.[21] However, the Geneva Convention was not the first attempt to protect people in occupied territories. The 1899 Hague Regulations insisted that occupiers may not 'forcibly transport or deport civilians' (Article 49) or compel civilians in occupied territories to work (Article 51), and were obliged to ensure that civilians enjoyed adequate food and medical supplies (Article 55). All these restrictions were breached during the Second World War. The debate at Geneva was framed largely by recent experience. Representatives of formerly occupied states called for wide-ranging rights for the inhabitants of occupied territories, including a right to launch insurgencies against the occupiers. Others, particularly the US and UK – in the post-war world occupiers themselves – and recently decolonized states, argued that placing too many restrictions on occupiers would provide succour to guerrillas, terrorists and rioters and make it impossible to govern effectively.[22]

Together the 1949 Convention and 1977 Additional Protocols constitute a comprehensive set of regulations limiting what the victors are entitled to do to civilians in occupied territories. It is worth mentioning the key principles as collated into a single body of law by the British Ministry of Defence.[23] Among many other things, the law insists that all people be treated humanely and specifically prohibits murder, torture, corporal punishment and mutilation, the taking of hostages, collective punishments, humiliating and degrading treatment and threats to commit any of these acts (paras 9.3 and 9.4). Civilians enjoy a wide range of rights relating to trial and punishment, including basic rights to fair trials and legal representation (para. 9.6). Women and children are to receive special respect and care (paras 9.8 and 9.9) and humanitarian agencies must be granted free passage (paras 9.12 and 9.13). Given that these legal regulations share a basic starting point with the minimalist approach to *jus post bellum* (constraining the victors) it is fair to surmise that whatever other acts may be justified by reference to the just cause for war, it is impermissible to breach these legal requirements.

The second problem is what should happen after unjust wars. Walzer rightly argues that the legitimacy of the war and that of the peace be regarded as two separate questions. He argues that while an unjust peace may undermine an otherwise just war, an unjust war cannot be legitimated by instituting a just peace.[24] With one eye clearly on Iraq, Walzer maintains that it is possible that a premature act of pre-emption or a misguided military intervention might topple a tyrannical regime. In such circumstances, although the war itself would remain unjust and a just peace would not retrospectively change its normative status, the peace might still become just in itself.[25] While this argument certainly answers the question of the unjust victor by positing a separate *jus post bellum* test, it does so at the risk of harming the initial rationale of the minimalist approach – of unifying the legitimacy of war and the peace on the grounds that just wars are wars waged to secure a just peace.

If we accept this, the problem for the minimalist becomes one of finding the criteria for evaluating the peace. Recall that, for minimalists, the scope of the *jus post bellum* is set by the just cause for war. If we deny in a particular instance that there was a just cause for war, minimalists are left bereft of criteria. Indeed, Walzer cannot make his argument without moving away from minimalism and importing two maximalist propositions: that victors have a responsibility to guarantee the security of people in occupied lands that goes beyond the legal to do no harm to civilians in occupied territories and that they have a responsibility to begin the political and economic reconstruction of the vanquished country.[26] This takes *jus post bellum* beyond the rights vindication endorsed by minimalists. For Walzer, the roots of this proposition come from democratic political theory which, he argues, ought to provide the 'central principles' for *jus post bellum*. As Walzer explains:

> [W]e want wars to end with governments in power in the defeated states that are chosen by the people they rule – or, at least, recognized by them as legitimate – and that are visibly committed to the welfare of those same people (all of them).[27]

Thus, while Walzer frames his theory of the peace around the idea of rights vindication and security, he cannot avoid making a maximalist argument – importing criteria from outside the just causes of war – to get around the problem of unjust wars.

After an unjust war, the victor remains obliged to treat civilians in accordance with the Geneva Conventions and Additional Protocols and commits war crimes if it fails to do so. But this legislation is partial, covering only the treatment of civilians in occupied territories. It says nothing about self-determination or economic restitution. On these wider matters, one cannot set forth criteria for just peace without stepping beyond the vindication of rights. If a war is manifestly unjust, therefore, the minimalist approach to *jus post bellum* does not offer any way of distinguishing better from worse beyond judgements about the treatment of civilians at the hands of the victorious soldiers. This issue is not unimportant but is far from comprehensive. We are forced in such situations either to call for immediate withdrawal to minimize the harm done or to revert to a maximalist position (see below).

The third problem relates to the ill fit between minimalism's concept of war and the actual war on terror. Minimalism is predicated on a singular understanding of war that is unsuited to the war on terror. Minimalists assume a Clausewitzian war between states waged over territory, economic rights or some other types of dispute (see Chapters 1 and 3). Although not yet obsolete, this type of war is now the exception rather than the rule and bears little resemblance to the war on terror. Even where aspects of the war on terror resemble traditional inter-state warfare, as in the invasion of Iraq, the aim has typically been to overthrow governments rather than impose our will on them or acquire territory and resources. Minimalism has little to say about the wars that occur within states or outside this traditional image of a contest between sovereigns.

The maximalist approach

This approach begins from the proposition that there is a 'presumption against war' in just war thinking and that the victors acquire special responsibilities towards the vanquished that go above and beyond that of not demanding more than is necessary to restore and secure the rights whose violation necessitated war in the first place.[28] According to the maximalist position, *jus post bellum* places additional burdens on combatants irrespective of whether their cause was just. Maximalists require that the victors take full responsibility for governing the vanquished in cases where the latter's government collapses as a result of war (a position endorsed by the 1949 Geneva Conventions) and take active measures to avoid sowing the seeds of future war by, for instance, assisting in the long-term economic reconstruction of the vanquished, as the US did with both Germany and Japan after 1945.

Afghanistan and Iraq have brought to the fore the question of the victors' responsibility to assume the reins of government. Indeed, some critics of the 2003 invasion of Iraq argued that it was America's failure to prepare for the peace that undermined the war's legitimacy. Certainly, there is something to be said for the claim that the numerous insurgencies that have confronted allied forces would have been lessened had the allies been more successful in rapidly improving the lives of ordinary Iraqis. Instead, across a range of indicators, including security and economic, the standard of living in Iraq is as bad as, if not worse in some areas, than it was under Saddam's tyranny.[29]

There is a broad consensus among theorists of *jus post bellum* that if a government falls as a result of a just war, then the victor acquires all the responsibilities of government. Some limit this requirement to cases where a war has been waged to end genocide, primarily because in such instances a failure to commit to reconstruction is indicative of an absence of genuine humanitarian intent behind the original intervention.[30] This position is broadly endorsed by Wheeler, who insists that it is an intervention's humanitarian outcomes, not its motivations, that primarily shape its legitimacy.[31] This idea also finds voice in the International Commission on Intervention and State Sovereignty's notion of a 'responsibility to rebuild' after armed intervention.[32]

An alternative perspective holds that the duty to assume the responsibilities of government is grounded in the changing nature of peacemaking. According to Stahn, at the outset of the twentieth

century wars were normally resolved either by bilateral or multilateral negotiation or were produced by the capitulation of one
or more of the attackers, resulting in conquest or occupation.[33]
Where wars were settled by negotiation, such negotiations usually
focused on the redistribution of territories, financial payments for
damages and the future control of armaments. Since 1945, however,
both types of war-ending have become rarer. On the one hand, a
significant body of law has developed prohibiting both the alteration
of borders by force and foreign rule, the latter under the commonly
accepted norm that sovereignty derives from the will of the people.[34]
On the other hand, it has become more common for international
institutions, ad hoc coalitions and individual states to intervene
as peacemakers. What might be labelled 'new peacemaking' goes
beyond measures designed to help belligerents reach compromise
and includes building political structures that respect human rights,
permit self-determination, punish wrongdoers and promote social,
economic and legal reconstruction.[35] This perspective, which is
implicitly founded on the view that peace should be understood
positively as the acquisition of certain societal goods (such as the
fulfilment of basic needs and rights, mechanisms for non-violent
conflict resolution, and an inclusive political and economic order),
insists that those who set themselves up as peacemakers acquire the
responsibility to help build positive peace.

Another way of approaching the question of transitional government from a maximalist perspective is to argue that the distinction
between occupation and the assumption of government based on
the 1907 Hague Regulations, so crucial to the minimalist case, is
obsolete. Benvenisti argues that there are three reasons why this is
so.[36] First, the expansion of the modern state and collective expectations of the state's role in society and the economy make it difficult
to distinguish areas of administration that should remain beyond
the scope of the authority bestowed upon the occupier. Indeed,
some commentators argue that even under the Hague Regulations,
occupiers were entitled to define almost any area of public policy as
necessary for the maintenance of public order, in practice enabling
them to legislate in any area in which they wished to intervene.[37]
In practice, by defining 'public order' broadly, occupiers went well

beyond simply tempering respect for the domestic law of the vanquished with international standards.

Second, Benvenisti argues that in practice occupiers have never behaved neutrally to the population of vanquished states, as appears to be required by minimalism. He argues that both prior to and during the Second World War, all the major belligerents violated the Hague Regulations. Britain, for example, dismissed the regulations by pointing to recognition of governments other than the one wielding administrative authority, the conclusion of separate agreements with 'local elements', and legalized claims to sovereign authority (obtained through 'unconditional surrender') in vanquished enemy states.[38] This suggests to Benvenisti that the Hague Regulations did not attain the status of customary law and should therefore not guide reflection on the legitimacy of the peace.

The third problem with the distinction between occupation and government that is central to the minimalist approach lies in its assumption that the protection of the civilian population involves the preservation of sovereign authority in its pre-war condition. In fact the minimalist approach seems to suggest that this assumption cannot be an absolute for – as we saw earlier – it permits the removal of a government and transformation of a state and society in cases where the nature of the state and/or society themselves give just cause for war. A narrow reading of the Hague Regulations suggests, however, that if the will of the people and sovereign authority of the people collide, then the occupier is duty bound to protect the latter, not the former. This idea had its roots in colonial politics as the Great Powers amassed at The Hague shared an interest in legitimating colonial rule.[39] They agreed that if an enemy state is entirely extinguished, sovereign authority passes to the victor with no regard for the will of the people. This argument, Benvenisti shows,[40] was also used to justify colonial reoccupation in the latter stages of the Second World War.

If the distinction between occupation and the assumption of the reins of government is untenable but it is still agreed that occupying forces have a responsibility to protect civilians in their care, then it follows that victors have a responsibility to assume transitional authority. Benvenisti argues[41] that this shift is evident in the differences between the Hague Regulations and the fourth Geneva Convention, though the distinction between Hague law and Geneva law is not a clear proxy for the distinction between minimalism and maximalism. He suggests that the Convention places the protection of the civilian population ahead of the preservation of sovereign authority, pointing as evidence to Article 47, which insists that the occupants of occupied territories must not be deprived of their rights. The meaning of this distinction could be read as supporting either the minimalist view (it restrains the victors from violating rights) or maximalist case (it creates positive duties to assume transitional government).

Benvenisti also argues that the Convention affords occupiers many more duties and rights than the Regulations. While many of these stipulations (such as the duty to treat people humanely, Article 27) could be read in support of either perspective, others – in particular the duty to facilitate the care for and education of children (Article 51), the duty to ensure medical and food supplies (Article 56) and the obligation to enable relief schemes (Article 59) – create duties that go beyond the duty to restrain the behaviour of victorious soldiers towards civilian populations. While a minimalist case could no doubt be made for each of these additional duties, the overall intention behind them is to create duties beyond the duty to limit post-war policy to rights vindication within the bounds of commonly accepted human rights. There are at least two reasons for thinking this. First, the Convention itself contains a mechanism authorizing the occupying power to repeal or suspend the law of the occupied territory if it constitutes a 'threat to security' or undermines the Convention's application (Article 64). This article alone suggests that the Convention means its provisions to be read as positive ('a responsibility to') not negative ('a responsibility not to inhibit') duties. Second, the records of the drafting process demonstrate that these additional responsibilities were understood at the time as positive duties and were therefore deeply controversial. For instance, reflecting on these clauses Albert Clattenberg, chair of the US experts' delegation to the 1947 conference that laid the foundations for the Convention, complained that:

The state of mind of the delegates of the liberated countries described above led in the first place to the making of wholly impractical suggestions almost as though it were believed that legislation could make the lot of conquered peoples and other victims pleasant ... ; as a Chinese Red Cross delegate is reputed to have said the previous summer, the cure for all China's problems would be to have new conventions along these lines and then to persuade some other powers to occupy the entire country.[42]

The point here is that a maximalist case can be made by reference to the prevailing law of occupation which, by this reading, insists that victors are obliged to do more than simply refrain from unduly harming the vanquished.

In summary, the maximalist case begins from the position that because war always produces bad consequences, victors have a moral and legal obligation to do more afterwards than merely satisfy their own rights. They must also remove the seeds of potential future war by punishing those guilty of initiating aggressive war and positively assisting the civilian population in building legitimate and peaceful government institutions and rebuilding the domestic economy. While some variants of maximalism suggest that these additional duties accrue only after certain types of war (such as war against a genocidal state), others insist that the responsibilities exist after all types of war when the government has collapsed. This begs the additional question of what responsibilities a victor has towards enemy civilians if the vanquished state does not collapse, especially where the vanquished state was both the cause of war and a persistent violator of its citizens' rights. Iraq 1991 is a case in point. For some commentators at the time, the US-led coalition had a moral responsibility to overthrow Saddam's regime both in order to remove a threat to regional security and protect the rights of Iraqi citizens.[43]

Just peace in the war on terror

Given the preceding discussion, what would a just peace for the war on terror look like? Answering this involves a different sort of analysis from that of the previous chapters because it is inherently forward-looking and speculative and because the two positions set out above do not enjoy the same historical pedigree as those outlined in Chapter 1. Nevertheless, it is possible to determine some basic principles and use these to evaluate the extent to which the different components of the war on terror are forging a just peace.

My first observation is that we cannot evaluate the peace potentially delivered by the war on terror as a single good, because the war on terror cannot be morally justified except by reference to its specific elements, including the wars in Afghanistan and Iraq. It is important, therefore, to take each aspect of the war on terror on its own merits, while observing that the claim that the war on terror as a whole can contribute towards a global just peace makes little moral or logical sense, for the reasons set out in Chapter 3. For space reasons, I will focus my comments on Afghanistan and Iraq.

Afghanistan Both minimalist and maximalist claims are plausible in relation to Afghanistan because of the connections with 9/11. The minimalist line would maintain that because Operation Enduring Freedom was an act of self-defence, the US was entitled to use force to neutralize that threat. If doing so necessarily involved the collapse or destruction of the Afghan government, then the US acquired the legal responsibilities set out in the laws of occupation but had no further special responsibilities to assist the people of Afghanistan. In other words, although it might make prudent policy to assist in the economic, political and social reconstruction of Afghanistan, from the minimalist point of view the US was not morally required to do so because it was engaging in a war of self-defence. Critics on the left disputed this view, arguing that the use of force against Afghanistan was, at best, imprudent. In terms of the approach to self-defence set out in Chapter 4, it is clear that the US did have moral grounds for intervening in Afghanistan. It is worth noting that prior to intervening, the US demanded that the Taliban suppress Al Qaeda and hand over those responsible for the 9/11 atrocities. Only when the Taliban refused did the coalition intervene.

The US has adopted a 'hands-off' approach to the rebuilding of Afghanistan while focusing its military operations on ongoing activities against those Al Qaeda and Taliban forces associated with the 9/11 attacks. The result has been the so-called 'light footprint' approach to post-war reconstruction (see below).

When the Taliban collapsed in late 2001, the US moved quickly to divest itself of responsibility for rebuilding. Instead, it called for the UN to assume responsibility for post-war reconstruction and, after some initial reluctance, encouraged NATO to take the lead in maintaining the peace in Afghanistan. Meanwhile, US forces focused on continuing their counter-insurgency against the remnants of Al Qaeda and the Taliban. Amongst America's allies there was – and remains – little stomach for a large-scale, protracted engagement such as that seen in post-war Germany and Japan or, more recently, in the Balkans. On the one hand, it was widely recognized that Afghans would be much less receptive to heavy external interference than East Timorese, Bosnians or Kosovars. On the other hand, governments had little interest in a major commitment to Afghanistan, and the US itself was initially concerned that a large international presence in Afghanistan might hinder its ongoing military operations against the Taliban and Al Qaeda. A different approach to post-conflict reconstruction that involved a minimal international presence was needed.

The baton was passed to the UN's Special Representative for Afghanistan, Lakhdar Brahimi. Taking up his new job in October 2001, Brahimi insisted that 'the UN is not seeking a transitional administration or peacekeeping or anything like that' in Afghanistan. Instead, the principal aim of this new model was to bring Afghan parties together and assist them in rebuilding their country.[44] This was known as the 'light footprint' approach, an approach that has much in common with the minimalist take on *jus post bellum*. The guiding principle was that the UN and other international actors should focus on bolstering local capacity with as small an international staff as possible.[45] Its advocates argued that it avoided the appearance of neo-colonialism, was much less expensive than a full-blown transitional administration, and guaranteed that the occupiers would not overstep the mark of what they were legitimately entitled to do. From this point of view, the light footprint acknowledged the wider needs of reconstruction without advocating the wholesale assumption of government and its attendant costs and moral problems. Moreover, assuming that the local authorities enjoyed the support of the host population – a problematic assumption given the central government's limited influence in Afghanistan's provinces – this approach is intended to leave behind more legitimate political structures than the alternative because they have been built and shaped by indigenous political leaders.[46]

The light footprint involves using international agencies to accomplish tasks such as the provision of security in some major cities, capacity building support for the state bureaucracy and training and equipping a national army and police service, while permitting indigenous leaders to develop their own preferred type of polity and retain ownership of the overall rebuilding process. In sharp contrast to operations such as those in the Balkans and East Timor, where international actors assumed the full responsibilities and authorities of government, international agencies in Afghanistan did not insist upon the institution of a particular form of democracy and government. Instead they left these decisions to tribal elders in the Loya Jirga – a traditional Afghan forum for deliberation and collective decision-making. So long as certain basic conditions were satisfied (some form of democracy, an open economy, respect for basic human rights), international agencies were prepared to allow the Afghan government to control and direct the rebuilding effort.[47]

There are clear advantages to the light footprint. Not least, in theory it is consistent with the minimalist view that the victors be constrained by the terms of their just cause and the laws of occupation. Moreover, its underlying principle that the purpose of international engagement is to facilitate the development of sustainable local capacity is very appealing. However, there are also a number of key problems which suggest a potential correlation between the limited international engagement with Afghan reconstruction and the recent resurgence of the Taliban which has necessitated a renewed military engagement on the part of NATO and – in some regions at least – an almost full-scale resumption of hostilities.

First, by placing authority in the hands of local elites, the light footprint approach runs the risk of legitimizing warlords and embedding tyranny. There is a danger that it could contribute to the creation of cultures of impunity and leave intact the basic social, military and economic structures that gave rise to the Taliban and its alliance with Al Qaeda in the first place. For instance, one of the key partners in peace in Afghanistan was General Dostum's 'Northern Alliance'. Dostum was a notorious war criminal whose bloody career included several massacres of civilians and prisoners. By working with, rather than working to replace, the existing structures in Afghanistan, the US and its allies might be leaving the seeds of future confrontation intact.

This is still entirely consistent with a minimalist perspective. However, maximalists would argue that because war must aim to establish a just and sustainable peace, it is incumbent on the occupiers to tear down the social structures that sowed the seeds of extremism and terrorism and replace them with more peaceful structures. This is not to say that the maximalist course would not be difficult, expensive and riddled with its own moral and instrumental problems connected to imposing one set of values on a society where a very different set prevails. But it would be foolhardy to deny that the persistence of violent and radical groups in Afghanistan and the resurgence of violence is partly due to the fact that despite the institution of a new government in Kabul, the underlying structures that caused and fed violent radicalism in Afghanistan have remained intact outside the capital.

Second, comparative figures for Kosovo and Afghanistan demonstrate that the light footprint can serve as a cover for chronic underinvestment and a much reduced level of engagement. In Afghanistan, the light footprint approach to security has enabled the resurgence of the Taliban and has produced only 'modest gains' in relation to economic growth, education and infrastructure. According to one estimate the approach cost $52 per capita in the first two years, whereas the transitional administration in Kosovo cost $814 per capita over the same period.[48] In other words, the minimalist approach might serve as a convenient way of justifying why the average Kosovar has received sixteen times the amount of reconstruction assistance afforded to the average Afghan. Given this, it is not surprising that international agencies and the Afghan government have failed to revive the economy, a factor that has, no doubt, contributed to the growth in the opium trade in the past few years. As RAND, one of America's leading military research institutes, concluded: 'low input of military and civilian resources yields low output in terms of security, democratic transformation, and economic development'.[49]

The case of Afghanistan shows that it is difficult to identify precisely the moral components of a just peace. At first glance, the light footprint approach seems a morally consistent and carefully limited minimalist way of dealing with the problem. It recognizes that the US and its allies were entitled to wage war on Al Qaeda and the Taliban in order to remove the extant threat they posed and that they did not accrue special responsibilities for Afghanistan beyond those set out in the laws of occupation. Moreover, the focus on self-determination and Afghan institutions sits comfortably with our liberal disposition towards self-rule and cultural plurality and discomfort with foreign imposition. But on closer inspection, the light footprint is producing some troubling effects. By failing to tackle the underlying structural causes of Afghan radicalism, it is failing to build a more just and stable peace – witnessed by the fact that in the last year or so Afghanistan has become decidedly *less* peaceful. What is more, the minimalist approach helps justify minimal reconstruction supported by insufficient resources.

So it would seem that Afghanistan might support the case for maximalism. Having overthrown the Taliban in a war of self-defence, the US and its allies acquired responsibilities for the future political, social and economic well-being of Afghanistan and a special responsibility for ensuring that the Afghanistan they leave behind is a more just and less radicalized country than the Afghanistan they found. If that is so, the expanded military commitment seen in the last couple of years is to be applauded but needs augmenting with a properly resourced plan to transform the Afghan polity and economy.

Iraq The morality of the 'peace' in Iraq – such as it is – is made more complex because, as I argued in Chapter 4, the war in Iraq was unjust. Because of such cases it is important to maintain a distinction between the justice of the war and the justice of the peace. Conflating the two would force us to insist that every act of violence committed by coalition forces in Iraq was unjust because they had no moral right to be there, let alone using violence. A moral framework that forced us into this position would very quickly become an irrelevance. What is more, it is naïve to think that Iraq today would be best served by an immediate withdrawal of coalition forces. A substantial proportion of the various militia groups in Iraq have quasi-genocidal ambitions and have demonstrated their intent and ability to kill non-combatants in large numbers. There are very good reasons for thinking that a precipitate withdrawal from Iraq would quickly be followed by massive bloodshed and ethnic cleansing, even genocide, as the various groups reoriented the distribution of territory on sectarian lines.

Several human rights organizations, including International Crisis Group (ICG) – no friend of the Bush administration – have also come to this conclusion and have written detailed reports powerfully setting out their case. For instance, the ICG found that 'the forces that dominate the current government thrive on identity politics, communal polarisation and a cycle of intensifying violence and counter-violence ... political leaders are becoming warlords'.[50] In 2007, Gareth Evans, president of the ICG and member of former UN Secretary-General Kofi Annan's 'High-Level Panel', argued that Iraq was in real danger of descending into genocide and mass atrocities.[51] In comparison with this large body of evidence and analysis, there is little other than wishful thinking to support the view that rapid withdrawal would produce an outbreak of peace.

It is therefore clear that we cannot apply the minimalist account of *jus post bellum* to the Iraq case, the main reason being that because the war itself was unjust, there are no 'just causes' that need to be fulfilled that can guide our moral judgements. Also, the minimalist requirement that unjust victors minimize their wrongdoing by withdrawing as quickly as possible while complying with the laws of occupation is, in this case, likely to produce a morally worse outcome because precipitate withdrawal is likely to enable the commission of genocide and mass atrocities by one or more of the rival Iraqi factions. We therefore need a maximalist account of *jus ad bellum* to work out what is owed, morally speaking, to Iraq.

Maximalism requires that the victors take responsibility for building stable peace, replete with a functioning and legitimate polity and thriving and sustainable economy. Some progress has been made towards achieving this goal. The US-led coalition adopted a novel approach to state building that attempted to democratize the process by holding early elections to determine who would play a role in constitution-writing. Although commendable in principle, because it implied a rapid transition to democratic rule and granted ownership of the process to the Iraqis themselves, this model left the process open to political factionalism and created an opening for radicals and spoilers to shape the structure of government and chronically delay progress. This is precisely what has happened. Individual ministries have become personal fiefdoms, particularly in some of the provinces but also in some of the large cities such as Baghdad and Basra, where the police forces in particular have been heavily infiltrated by the factions and often serve factional interests more than they uphold the rule of law. What is more, factionalism has inhibited the development of consensus on issues such as the constitution and has often left the Iraqi government hamstrung and blocked at every turn.

There have been numerous suggestions as to how to go about remedying this problem – ranging from the partition of Iraq to effectively starting all over again and recognizing that some elements of the Iraqi government have themselves become part of the problem. This is not the place to pick through the specifics of these different proposals. The point here is simply to reinforce the argument that the occupying forces have a moral responsibility to help Iraq build a legitimate and effective political system and that – to date – this process has not been going terribly well. Nevertheless, contrary to what commentators on both the left and right of politics seem to think, the failure of past initiatives – even if these were caused by Iraqi politicians and factional leaders – does not exhaust the occupier's moral responsibility. The coalition has a moral responsibility to build a legitimate and effective political system, a responsibility divested only when Iraq *has* such a system. To put it another way, it would be immoral to withdraw or scale back the commitment to Iraq before such a system had been created. It may seem counter-intuitive for me to argue against rapid withdrawal, having insisted that the war itself was immoral. But the choice facing the coalition is whether it wants to compound its unjust war with an unjust and unstable peace or whether it wants partly to redeem itself by building a just peace. My view is that *jus post bellum* creates a moral obligation to do the latter.

Reports suggest that, if anything, the effort to rebuild the Iraqi economy, restore basic human services and maintain security – other planks of the maximalist account of *jus post bellum* – have been more shambolic than the effort to build a political system. Corruption and inefficiency are rife and the coalition failed to restore and then maintain basic services. According to many reports, living conditions in many parts of Iraq are worse today than they were before the invasion.

The coalition's most famous failure has been in the area of security. It has failed to create a sufficiently secure environment, leaving Iraqis exposed to the danger of terrorism and thwarting efforts to rebuild the economy. The terrorists must take the blame for the carnage they wreak – just as coalition forces should be blamed and punished when they deliberately or recklessly kill non-combatants. However, according to the maximalist take on just peace, the occupying forces have a moral responsibility to protect Iraq's civilian population from terrorism. As is now well known, the US deployed too few forces to secure Iraq's borders and streets and acted too slowly to deal with the rising tide of terrorism. The poor state of security in Iraq makes it more difficult to achieve any of the other goals of post-war reconstruction. For our purposes, however, the important point is that the coalition had a moral responsibility to protect Iraqis, which it has failed to discharge.

It is therefore clear that – arguably despite its good intentions – the US-led coalition in Iraq is failing to build the just peace that it is morally required to do. There seems little sign that new strategies such as 'the surge' are likely to remedy this problem and it is distressing that not one of the presidential candidates has a plan for discharging America's moral responsibility by investing the political skill, time, energy and personnel in building a just peace. The mishandling of affairs since 2003 means that it is harder to build a just peace in Iraq now than it was immediately after the invasion, but this has no effect on what is required, morally speaking. As such, I am in the rather odd position of arguing that the invasion of Iraq was unjust but that what is needed is heightened, not lessened, engagement with building the peace.

This argument hits up against a powerful lesser evil argument – that because the coalition's presence in Iraq is illegitimate, it is doing more harm than good and should withdraw immediately. This is a plausible argument but is one based on the *hope* that withdrawal would be the lesser evil rather than evidence to this effect. At the time of writing, this is an assessment I do not share. The withdrawal of the minimal protection offered by coalition forces would, I fear, leave Iraqi civilians exposed to the worst excesses of the radicals and terrorists. By my understanding of the situation in Iraq, the current status quo, not a projected withdrawal, is the lesser expected evil. However, that does not mean that the coalition should not do more to legitimize its status. Bringing the UN more fully on board and transferring authority and command to the global body may be one way of doing this, though the UN's caution and sometimes downright hostility to taking on a role such as this is well placed given recent history. Behaving more cautiously and legitimately inside Iraq might be another good place to start.

Conclusion

The ethics of war need to take account of the moral quality of the peace. In this chapter, I have set out two approaches to evaluating the morality of the peace and used these to examine the justice of the peace in Afghanistan and Iraq. It is clear that much more needs to be done before the US and its allies can claim to be building a just peace. First and foremost, they need to forget the language of an overarching war on terror and set out clear moral justifications for each of their military actions. Because the war on terror is amorphous, it is virtually impossible to explore whether it is capable of building a just peace and what that just peace might look like. Certainly, the discussion in Chapter 3 suggests that such a peace is not possible. It is clear that both Afghanistan and Iraq have a long way to go and there is a pattern of indifference to building long-term stable peace on the part of the anti-terror allies. This indifference could ultimately undermine the very purposes of the war on terror. This is a major problem because, after all, the ultimate moral test of war is the quality of the peace we leave behind.

Notes

Introduction

1 David Keen, *Endless War? Hidden Functions of the 'War on Terror'* (London: Pluto, 2006).

2 Ken Booth and Nicholas J. Wheeler, *The Security Dilemma: Fear, Cooperation and Trust in World Politics* (London: Palgrave, 2008), pp. 3–4.

3 The anchorage metaphor is taken from Ken Booth, *Theory of World Security* (Cambridge: Cambridge University Press, 2007), pp. 235–6.

4 For instance, James Turner Johnson, *The War to Oust Saddam Hussein: Just War and the Face of New Conflict* (Lanham, MD: Rowman and Littlefield, 2005).

1 Ethics and war

1 'Israel Soldiers Killed Near Lebanon', *BBC News*, 7 October 2003.

2 William T. Sherman, *Memoirs of General William T. Sherman: By Himself* (Bloomington: Indiana University Press, 1957 [1875]), p. 660.

3 Edward Hagerman, 'Union Generalship, Political Leadership and Total War Strategy', in Stig Förster and Jörg Nagler (eds), *On the Road to Total War: The American Civil War and the German Wars of Unification, 1861–1871* (Cambridge:

Cambridge University Press, 1997), p. 166.

4 'Blair Calls for Unity', *BBC News*, 21 March 2003.

5 Thucydides, *History of the Peloponnesian War*, translated by Rex Warner (Harmondsworth: Penguin, 1972).

6 Machiavelli, *The Prince*, translated by W. K. Marriott (London: Dent, 1958).

7 Carl von Clausewitz, *On War*, edited and translated by Michael Howard and Peter Paret (London: Everyman's Library, 1993), p. 77.

8 Hans J. Morgenthau, *A New Foreign Policy for the United States* (Washington, DC: Council on Foreign Relations, 1969), pp. 134–8; John J. Mearsheimer and Stephen Walt, 'An Unnecessary War', *Foreign Policy*, 134, 2003.

9 Josiah Ober, 'Classical Greek Times', in Michael Howard, George J. Andreopoulos and Mark R. Shulman (eds), *The Laws of War: Constraints on Warfare in the Western World* (New Haven, CT: Yale University Press, 1994), pp. 12–26.

10 Immanuel Kant, *Perpetual Peace: A Philosophical Essay* (1795), translated by M. Campbell Smith (London: Simon Sonnenschein & Co., 1903).

11 Michael Ignatieff, *The Lesser Evil: Political Ethics in an Age of Terror* (Edinburgh: Edinburgh University Press, 2004).

12 Christopher Coker, 'The War on Ethics', public lecture to the University of Queensland Conflict and Security Research Group, 2007.

13 Richard Holmes, *On War and Morality* (Princeton, NJ: Princeton University Press, 1989).

14 George Weigel, 'The Development of Just War Thinking in the Post-Cold War World: An American Perspective', in Charles Reed and David Ryall (eds), *The Price of Peace: Just War in the Twenty-first Century* (Cambridge: Cambridge University Press, 2007), p. 29.

15 Natan Sharansky, 'Democracy for Peace', American Enterprise Institute for Public Policy Research, World Forum, Washington, DC, 20 June 2002.

16 Cited in Stephen A. Garrett, *Ideals and Reality: An Analysis of the Debate Over Vietnam* (Washington, DC: University Press of America, 1978), p. 153.

17 Tom Farer, 'Legal and Legitimate Use of Force: The UN Charter and the Neoconservative Challenge', Background Paper No. 1, *Carnegie Council*, 2006, p. 11.

18 E. H. Carr, *The Twenty Years Crisis 1919–1939: An Introduction to the Study of International Relations* (London: Macmillan, 1960).

19 John Stuart Mill, 'A Few Words on Non-Intervention' [1859], in John Stuart Mill, *Essays on Politics and Culture*, edited by Gertrude Himmelfarb (Gloucester: Peter Smith, 1973), pp. 368–84.

20 Jean Bethke Elshtain, 'Terrorism', in Charles Reed and David Ryall (eds), *The Price of Peace: Just War in the Twenty-first Century* (Cambridge: Cambridge University Press, 2007), p. 131.

21 See John Kelsay, 'Islamic Tradition and the Justice of War', in Torkel Brekke (ed.), *The Ethics of War in Asian Civilizations: A Comparative Perspective* (London: Routledge, 2006), pp. 92–3.

22 Steven Ratner, 'Are the Geneva Conventions Out of Date?', *Law Quadrangle Notes*, summer 2005, p. 68.

23 Steven Forde, 'Classical Realism', in T. Nardin and D. R. Mapel (eds), *Traditions of International Ethics* (Cambridge: Cambridge University Press, 1993), p. 79.

24 Attorney General John Ashcroft, 'Preserving Our Freedoms While Defending Against Terrorism', Hearing before the Senate Committee on the Judiciary, 107th Congress, 2001.

25 Cited by Anthony Lewis, 'Making Torture Legal', *New York Review*, 15 (12), 15 July 2004, p. 2.

26 A. C. Grayling, *Among the Dead Cities: Was the Allied Bombing of Civilians in WWII a Necessity or a Crime?* (London: Bloomsbury, 2006).

27 H. Carpenter (ed.), *The Letters of J. R. R. Tolkien* (London: HarperCollins, 1995). Emphasis added.

28 Audrey Kurth Cronin, 'How al-Qaida Ends: The Decline and Demise of Terrorist Groups', *International Security*, 31 (1), 2006, pp. 7–48.

29 This section draws on Paul D. Williams, 'Security Studies, 9/11 and the Long War', in Alex J. Bellamy, Roland Bleiker, Sara E. Davies

and Richard Devetak (eds), *Security and the War on Terror* (London: Routledge, 2007).

30 Terence K. Kelly, 'The Just Conduct of War Against Radical Islamic Terror and Insurgencies', in Charles Reed and David Ryall (eds), *The Price of Peace: Just War in the Twenty-first Century* (Cambridge: Cambridge University Press, 2007), p. 204.

31 The following brief overview draws its argument and some of its text from the lengthier discussion in Alex J. Bellamy, *Just Wars: From Cicero to Iraq* (Cambridge: Polity, 2006).

32 Michael Walzer, *Just and Unjust Wars: A Moral Argument with Historical Illustrations* (New York: Basic Books, 1977), p. 59.

33 Paul Ramsey, *War and the Christian Conscience: How Shall Modern War be Conducted Justly?* (Durham, NC: Duke University Press, 1961), pp. 43, 48–9.

34 Walzer, *Just and Unjust Wars*, p. 156.

35 See Reed and Ryall (eds), *Price of Peace*.

36 Cronin, 'How al-Qaida Ends'.

2 What's wrong with terrorism?

1 Peter Kornbluh, 'Nicaragua: US Proinsurgency Warfare Against the Sandanistas', in Michael T. Klare and Peter Kornbluh (eds), *Low-Intensity Warfare: Counterinsurgency, Proinsurgency and Antiterrorism in the Eighties* (New York: Pantheon, 1988), p. 140.

2 See Philip Jenkins, *Ages of Terror: What We Can and Can't*

Know About Terrorism (New York: Aldine de Gruyter, 2003), p. 26.

3 Ibid.

4 See Paul Elliott, *Brotherhoods of Fear: A History of Violent Organizations* (London: Cassell, 1998), p. 104; Walter Laqueur, *The New Terrorism: Fanaticism and the Arms of Mass Destruction* (London: Phoenix Press, 1999), pp. 14–17.

5 See John Dugard, 'International Terrorism: Problems of Definition', *International Affairs*, 50 (1), 1974, pp. 67–81.

6 David Rodin, 'Terrorism without Intention', *Ethics*, 114 (4), 2004, p. 753.

7 See C. A. J. Coady, 'The Morality of Terrorism', *Philosophy*, 60, January 1985, pp. 47–68.

8 Bruce Hoffman, *Inside Terrorism* (New York: Columbia University Press, 1998), pp. 15–28.

9 Cited by Naji Abi-Hashem, 'Peace and War in the Middle East: A Pyschopolitical and Sociocultural Perspective', in Fathali M. Moghaddam and Anthony J. Marsella (eds), *Understanding Terrorism: Psychosocial Roots, Consequences and Interventions* (Washington, DC: American Psychological Association, 2004), p. 71.

10 Frederick J. Hacker, *Crusaders, Criminals, Crazies: Terror and Terrorism in Our Time* (New York: W. W. Norton and Company, 1976).

11 Walter Laqueur, 'Left, Right and Beyond: The Changing Face of Terror', in J. Hoge Jnr and G. Rose (eds), *How Did This Happen? Terrorism and the New War* (Oxford: Public Affairs, 2001), p. 80.

12 Andrew Silke, 'Becoming a

Terrorist', in Andrew Silke (ed.), *Terrorists, Victims and Society: Psychological Perspectives on Terrorism and Its Consequences* (London: Wiley, 2003), p. 32.

13 Rex A. Hudson, *Who Becomes a Terrorist and Why: The 1999 Government Report on Profiling Terrorists* (Guilford, CT: Lyons Press, 2000), pp. 40–8.

14 Article 1 (2), stated that '"acts of terrorism" means criminal acts directed against a state and intended or calculated to create a state of terror in the minds of … the general public'. The convention is reproduced in M. Cherif Bassiouni, *International Terrorism: Multilateral Conventions (1937–2001)*, (New York: Transnational Publishers, 2001), pp. 71–8.

15 See, for instance, David J. Whittaker, *Terrorism: Understanding the Global Threat* (London: Longman, 2002), p. 10; Hoffman, *Inside Terrorism* ((New York: Columbia University Press, 1998), p. 43; and A. J. Coates, *The Ethics of War* (Manchester: Manchester University Press, 1998), pp. 123–7.

16 Jean Bethke Elshtain, 'How to Fight a Just War', in Ken Booth and Tim Dunne (eds), *Worlds in Collision: Terror and the Future of Global Order* (Basingstoke: Palgrave Macmillan, 2002), p. 264.

17 Robert Goodin, *What's Wrong with Terrorism?* (Cambridge: Polity, 2006).

18 Cited in Arno J. Mayer, *The Furies: Violence and Terror in the French and Russian Revolutions* (Princeton, NJ: Princeton University Press, 2002), pp. 190–1.

19 Mona Ozouf, 'Jacobins: Fortune et Infortune d'un mot', in *L'école de la France: Essais sur la Révolution, L'utopia et L'enseignment* (Paris, 1984), p. 242.

20 David Garrioch, 'Revolutionary Violence and Terror in the Paris Sections', in Robert Aldrich and Martin Lyons (eds), *The Sphinx in the Tuileries* (Sydney: University of Sydney, 1999), pp. 67–76.

21 Turner Johnson, *Ideology, Reason and the Limitation of War* (Princeton, NJ: Princeton University Press, 1975), pp. 43–5.

22 Colm McKeogh, *Innocent Civilians: The Morality of Killing in War* (London: Palgrave, 2002), pp. 7–11.

23 Douglas Lackey, *The Ethics of War and Peace* (Englewood Cliffs, NJ: Prentice Hall, 1989), p. 85.

24 Gerry Wallace, 'Area Bombing, Terrorism and the Death of Innocents', in Brenda Almond and Donald Hill (eds), *The Ethics of Killing* (London: Routledge, 1991), p. 129.

25 Ibid., p. 132.

26 H. Khatchadourian, *The Morality of Terrorism* (London: Peter Lange, 1998), pp. 75–6.

27 Robert Young, 'Political Terrorism as a Weapon of the Politically Powerless', in Tony Coady and Michael O'Keefe (eds), *Terrorism and Justice*, pp. 24–5.

28 Virginia Held, 'Terrorism, Rights and Political Goals', in R. G. Frey and Christopher W. Morris (eds), *Violence, Terrorism and Justice* (Cambridge: Cambridge University Press, 1991), p. 62.

29 Ibid., p. 63.

30 See David J. Whittaker,

Terrorists and Terrorism in the Contemporary World (London: Routledge, 2004), pp. 108–9.

31 Saul Smilansky, 'Terrorism, Justification and Illusion', *Ethics*, 114 (4), 2004, p. 791.

32 Michael Walzer, *Just and Unjust War: A Moral Argument with Historical Illustrations* (New York: Basic Books, 1977), p. 262.

33 Kai Nielsen, 'Violence and Terrorism: Its Uses and Abuses', in Burton M. Leiser (ed.), *Values in Conflict* (New York: Macmillan, 1981), pp. 435–49.

34 Ronald E. Santoni, *Sartre on Violence: Curiously Ambivalent* (University Park: Pennsylvania State University Press, 2003), p. 60.

35 Ibid., pp. 117–27.

36 This and subsequent quotes are taken from the English translation reproduced in Walter Laqueur and Yonah Alexander (eds), *Terrorism Reader* (New York: Meridian, 1987), pp. 73–5.

37 Burleigh Taylor Wilkins, *Terrorism and Collective Responsibility* (London: Routledge, 1992), p. 25.

38 Ibid., p. 29.

39 Ibid., p. 31.

40 Frantz Fanon, *The Wretched of the Earth* (Harmondsworth: Penguin, 1967).

41 Louis P. Pojman, 'The Moral Response to Terrorism and Cosmopolitanism', in J. Sterba (ed.), *Terrorism and International Justice* (Oxford: Oxford University Press), p. 142.

42 Khatchadourian, *The Morality of Terrorism*, pp. 84–5.

43 Walzer, *Just and Unjust Wars*, p. 251.

44 Ibid., pp. 254–5.

45 Ibid., p. 253.

46 Ibid., p. 268.

47 Cited by Martin Kramer, 'The Moral Logic of Hizballah', in Walter Reich (ed.), *Origins of Terrorism: Psychologies, Ideologies, Theologies, States of Mind* (Baltimore, MD: Johns Hopkins University Press, 2002), p. 145.

48 Alex J. Bellamy, 'Supreme Emergencies and the Protection of Non-Combatants in War', *International Affairs*, 80 (5), 2004, pp. 829–50.

49 Michael Walzer, 'Terrorism: A Critique of Excuses', in Michael Walzer, *Arguing About War* (New Haven, CT: Yale University Press, 2004), p. 54.

50 Cited by Mark Juergensmeyer, *Terror in the Mind of God: The Global Rise of Religious Violence* (Berkeley: University of California Press, 2000), p. 216.

51 Albert Bandura, 'The Role of Selective Moral Disengagement in Terrorism and Counterterrorism', in F. M. Moghaddam and A. J. Marsella (eds), *Understanding Terrorism* (Washington, DC: American Psychological Association, 2004), pp. 125–6.

52 ABC interview cited by P. L. Williams, *Al Qaeda: Brotherhood of Terror* (Parsippany, NJ: Alpha, 2002), p. 135.

3 A just war on terror?

1 George W. Bush, Address to a Joint Session of Congress and the American People, 20 September 2001.

2 See Jean Bethke Elshtain, 'How to Fight a Just War', in

Ken Booth and Tim Dunne (eds), *Worlds in Collision: Terror and the Future of Global Order* (Basingstoke: Palgrave Macmillan, 2002), pp. 263–9.

3 Bush, Address to a Joint Session of Congress and the American People.

4 Oliver O'Donovan, *The Just War Revisited* (Cambridge: Cambridge University Press, 2003), p. ix.

5 Carl von Clausewitz, *On War* (edited and translated by M. Howard and P. Paret), (Princeton, NJ: Princeton University Press, 1976).

6 See Paul Robinson (ed.), *The Just War in Comparative Perspective* (Aldershot: Ashgate, 2003).

7 J. T. Johnson, *Morality and Contemporary Warfare* (New Haven, CT: Yale University Press, 1999), p. 7.

8 Thomas Aquinas, *Summa Theologiae*, translated and edited by Daniel J. Sullivan (Chicago, IL: William Benton, 1941), part II, q. 40, art. 2, p. 578.

9 James Muldoon, *Popes, Lawyers and Infidels: The Church and the Non-Christian World, 1250–1550* (University Park: Pennsylvania State University Press, 1979), pp. 10–12.

10 Francisco de Vitoria, 'On the American Indians', in Anthony Pagden and Jeremy Lawrence (eds), *Vitoria: Political Writings* (Cambridge: Cambridge University Press, 1991), p. 288. Emphasis added.

11 Francisco de Vitoria, 'On Dietary Laws, or Self-Restraint', in Pagden and Lawrence, *Vitoria*, pp. 223–7.

12 S. J. Frederick and C. Copleston, *A History of Philosophy: Volume 3 Late Medieval and Renaissance Philosophy* (New York: Doubleday, 1993), p. 395.

13 Francisco Suárez, *Selections from Three Works*, translated and edited by G. Williams, A. Brown and J. Waldron (New York: Carnegie, 1944), p. 824.

14 Ibid.

15 Thomas Hobbes, *The Leviathan*, edited by E. Curley (Cambridge: Cambridge University Press, 1994).

16 This discussion draws on Terry Nardin, 'The Moral Basis of Humanitarian Intervention', *Ethics and International Affairs*, 16 (1), 2002, pp. 61–2.

17 Grotius, *De Jure Belli et Pacis*, book II, chapter 25, para. 8 (4).

18 Ibid., chapter 10, para. 90 (1).

19 Samuel von Pufendorf, *Of the Law of Nature and Nations*, translated and edited by C. H. Oldfather and W. A. Oldfather (Oxford: Clarendon Press, 1934).

20 Christian Wolff, *The Law of Nations Treated According to a Scientific Method*, translated by Joseph Drake (Oxford: Oxford University Press, 1934).

21 See Michael W. Doyle, 'The New Interventionism', *Metaphilosophy*, 32 (1/2), 2001, p. 214.

22 Emmerich de Vattel, *Le Droit des Gens ou Principes de la Loi Naturelle, appliqués a la Conduite et aux Affaires des Nations et des Souverains* (1758), translated by Charles G. Fenwick (Washington, DC: Carnegie Institution, 1916), p. 87.

23 Ibid., p. 131.

24 The label 'equalitarian' is Christian Reus-Smit's.

25 See Finnemore, *The Purpose of Intervention*, pp. 59–60 and J. A. R. Marriott, *The Eastern Question: An Historical Study in European Diplomacy* (Oxford: Clarendon Press, 1917).

26 Cited by Louis B. Sohn and Thomas Buergenthal, *International Protection of Human Rights* (Indianapolis, IN: Bobbs-Merrill, 1973), p. 158.

27 Cited by Simon Chesterman, *Just War or Just Peace?* (Oxford: Oxford University Press, 2001), p. 35.

28 Jutta Brunee and Stephen J. Toope, 'The Use of Force: International Law After Iraq', *International and Comparative Law Quarterly*, 53 (3), 2004, p. 800.

29 John Paul II, 'On Social Concern', in David J. O'Brien and Thomas A. Shannon (eds), *Catholic Social Thought: The Documentary Heritage* (New York: Orbis, 1992), pp. 37–9; and United States Catholic Conference, 'The Harvest of Justice is Sown in Peace', in Gerard F. Powers, Drew Christiansen and Robert T. Hennemeyer (eds), *Peacemaking: Moral and Policy Challenges for a New World* (Washington, DC: United States Catholic Conference, 1994), p. 315.

30 John Paul II, 'On Social Concern', p. 38.

31 Richard B. Miller, 'Humanitarian Intervention, Altruism, and the Limits of Casuistry', *Journal of Religious Ethics*, 28 (1), 2000, p. 20.

32 John Paul II, 'Address to the Diplomatic Corps', *Origins*, 22, 4 February 1993, p. 587.

33 United States Catholic Conference, 'The Harvest of Justice', p. 22.

34 Richard B. Miller, *Interpretations of Conflict: Ethics, Pacifism and the Just War Tradition* (Chicago, IL: University of Chicago Press, 1991).

35 James Turner Johnson, *Morality and Contemporary Warfare* (New Haven, CT: Yale University Press, 1999), p. 57.

36 Oliver O'Donovan, *The Just War Revisited* (Cambridge: Cambridge University Press, 2003), p. 23.

37 Jean Bethke Elshtain, *Just War Against Terror: The Burden of American Power in a Violent World* (New Jersey: Basic Books, 2003).

38 Human Security Centre, *Human Security Report 2005* (Vancouver: Human Security Centre, 2005).

39 Elshtain, *Just War Against Terror*, pp. 69–70.

40 Letter from the President of the United States to the Speaker of the House of Representatives and Pro Tempore of the Senate.

41 Hugo Grotius, cited by Terry Nardin, 'The Moral Basis of Humanitarian Intervention', Paper presented at the Symposium on the Norms and Ethics of Humanitarian Intervention, Center for Global Peace and Conflict Studies, University of California, Irvine, 26 May 2000, p. 8.

4 Is pre-emption legitimate?

1 Georg Schwarzenberger, 'The Fundamental Principles of International Law', *Recueil des Cours* (The Hague: Academy of International Law, 1955), pp. 195–383.

2 Anthony Clark Arend and R. J. Beck, *International Law and the Use of Force: Beyond the Charter Paradigm* (London: Routledge, 1993), p. 72.

3 Eric P. J. Myjer and Nigel D. White, 'The Twin Towers Attack: An Unlimited Right to Self-Defence?', *Journal of Conflict and Security Law*, 7 (1), 2002, pp. 5–17.

4 The restrictionist line is taken by, among others, Laurie Calhoun, 'Pre-emption and Paradox', *Global Change, Peace and Security*, 16 (3), 2004, pp. 197–210.

5 Richard Betts, 'Striking First: A History of Thankfully Lost Opportunities', *Ethics and International Affairs*, 17 (1), 2003, p. 18.

6 Emmerich de Vattel, *The Law of Nations or the Principles of Natural Law*, 1758, book III, para. 35.

7 Francisco Suarez, *Selections from Three Works: De Triplici Virtute Theologica, Fide, Spe et Charitate*, edited and translated by G. L. Williams (New York: Carnegie Classics on International Law, 1944), para. 4, section 1; Christian Wolff, *Jus Gentium*, translated by Joseph Drake (New York: Carnegie Classics on International Law, 1934), p. 804.

8 Hugo Grotius, *De Jure Belli et Pacis*, 1625, pp. 206–10.

9 The following section draws on insights from Abraham D. Sofaer, 'On the Necessity of Pre-emption', *European Journal of International Law*, 14 (2), 2003, p. 216, notes 24–6.

10 Grotius, *De Jure Belli*, p. 210.

11 Ibid., p. 549.

12 Ibid., pp. 224–5.

13 Samuel Pufendorf, *De Jure Naturae et Gentium*, 1672, p. 264.

14 Sofaer, 'On the Necessity of Pre-emption', p. 216, note 25.

15 Vattel, *The Law of Nations*, p. 308.

16 Ibid., p. 130.

17 Ibid., p. 308.

18 Frank Kellogg, Address of the Hon. Frank B. Kellogg, 28 April 1928, cited in the *Proceedings of the American Society of International Law*, 22, 1928, pp. 141–3.

19 Yoram Dinstein, *War, Aggression and Self-Defence* (Cambridge: Grotius Publications, 1988), p. 169.

20 See, for instance, Jean Combacau, 'The Exception of Self-Defence in UN Practice', in Antonio Cassese (ed.), *The Current Legal Regulation of the Use of Force* (Dordrecht: Martinus Nijhoff, 1986), pp. 9–37.

21 Thomas M. Franck, 'Who Killed Article 2(4)? or: Changing Norms Governing the Use of Force by States', *American Journal of International Law* 64 (4), 1970, pp. 809–37.

22 International Court of Justice, *Case Concerning Military and Paramilitary Activities in and Against Nicaragua* (Merits) (1986), ICJ Report, p. 103.

23 See Ian Brownlie, *International Law and the Use of Force by States* (Oxford: Oxford University Press, 1963).

24 International Court of Justice, *Military and Paramilitary Activities in and Against Nicaragua*, p. 14.

25 Hans Kelsen, 'Collective Security and Collective Self-Defence Under the Charter', *American*

Journal of International Law, 42 (3), 1948, p. 792

26 Cited by Guy Roberts, 'The Counterproliferation Self-Help Paradigm: A Legal Regime for Enforcing the Norm Prohibiting the Proliferation of Weapons of Mass Destruction', *Denver Journal of International Law and Policy*, 27 (3), 1999, pp. 483, 513.

27 J. L. Kunz, 'Individual and Collective Self-Defence in Article 51 of the Charter of the United Nations', *American Journal of International Law* 41 (4), 1947, p. 878.

28 See V. Cassim, W. Debevoise, H. Kailes and T. W. Thompson, 'The Definition of Aggression', *Harvard International Law Journal*, 16, 1975, pp. 607–8.

29 D. W. Bowett, *Self-Defence in International Law* (Manchester: Manchester University Press, 1958), pp. 191–2.

30 Anthony Clark Arend, 'International Law and the Pre-Emptive Use of Military Force', *The Washington Quarterly*, 26 (2), 2003, pp. 89–103.

31 Christine Gray, *International Law and the Use of Force* (Oxford: Oxford University Press, 2000), pp. 112–13.

32 United Nations Security Council Resolution 487 (1987).

33 John Yoo, 'Using Force', *University of Chicago Law Review*, 71 (3), 2004, p. 765.

34 The following discussion draws on the detailed account of the *Caroline* affair provided by Kenneth R. Stevens, *Border Diplomacy: The Caroline and Mcleod Affairs in Anglo-American-Canadian Rela-* *tions, 1837–1842* (Montgomery: University of Alabama Press, 2004).

35 Ibid., pp. 24–5.

36 Ibid., p. 35.

37 *The Caroline*. Letter from Mr Webster to Mr Fox (24 April 1841), *British and Foreign State Papers*, 1129, 1138.

38 Ibid.

39 Daniel Webster, 'Letter to Sir Henry Stephen Fox', in K. E. Shewmaker (ed.), *The Papers of Daniel Webster: Diplomatic Papers, Volume 1: 1841–1843* (Armidale, ME: University of New England Press, 1983), pp. 67–8.

40 See Ingrid Detter, *The Law of War*, 2nd edition (Cambridge: Cambridge University Press 2000), p. 86.

41 George W. Bush, Speech at Cincinnati, 7 October 2002, www.whitehouse.gov/news/ releases/2002/10/20021007-8.html, accessed 2 February 2005.

42 See Richard A. Clarke, *Against All Enemies: Inside America's War on Terror* (New York: Free Press, 2004), pp. 101–204.

43 Ivo Daalder, *The Use of Force in a Changing World: US and European Perspectives* (Washington, DC: Brookings Institution, 2002).

44 See Richard K. Betts, 'The Soft Underbelly of American Primacy: Tactical Advantages of Terror', *Political Science Quarterly*, 117 (1), 2002, p. 33.

45 Donald Rumsfeld, 'Remarks at Stakeout Outside ABC TV Studio', 28 October 2001, www. defenselink.mil/news/Oct2001/ t10292001_t1028sd3.html, accessed 3 February 2007.

46 *The National Security*

Strategy of the United States of America (Washington, DC: White House, 2002), p. 15.

47 Ibid.

48 Ibid.

49 See Michael Byers, 'Letting the Exception Prove the Rule', *Ethics and International Affairs*, 17 (1), 2003, p. 11.

50 Ian Johnstone, 'US–UN Relations After Iraq: The End of the World (Order), as We Know It?', *European Journal of International Law*, 15 (4), 2004, p. 832.

51 Michael Byers, 'Policing the High Seas: The Proliferation Security Initiative', *American Journal of International Law*, 98 (3), 2004, p. 541.

52 Cited by Stefan Halper and Jonathan Clarke, *America Alone: The Neo-Conservatives and the Global Order* (Cambridge: Cambridge University Press, 2004), p. 140.

53 George W. Bush, Speech at the West Point Graduation ceremony, 1 June 2002, www.whitehouse.gov/news/releases/2002/06/print/20020601–8html, accessed 5 February 2007.

54 S. R. Weisman, 'Pre-emption Evolves from an Idea to Official Action', *New York Times*, 23 March 2003, p. B1.

55 See Ivo Daalder and James M. Lindsay, *America Unbound: The Bush Revolution in Foreign Policy* (Washington, DC: Brookings Institution Press, 2003), p. 127.

56 Sofaer, 'On the Necessity of Pre-emption', p. 219.

57 See Brad Roberts, 'NBC-Armed Rogues: Is There a Moral Case for Pre-Emption?', in Elliott

Abrams (ed.), *Close Calls: Intervention, Terrorism, Missile Defense, and 'Just War' Today* (Washington, DC: Ethics and Public Policy Center, 1998), pp. 103–4.

58 Jonathan I. Charney, 'The Use of Force Against Terrorism and International Law', *American Journal of International Law*, 95 (4), 2001, p. 835.

59 Myers S. McDougal and Florentino P. Feliciano, *Law and Minimum World Public Order: The Legal Regulation of International Coercion* (New Haven, CT: Yale University Press, 1961), p. 231.

60 *Financial Times*, 27 September 2002.

61 Michael Byers, 'Pre-emptive Self-Defence: Hegemony, Equality and Strategies of Legal Change', *Journal of Political Philosophy*, 11 (2), 2003, pp. 171–90.

62 See Neta C. Crawford, 'The Slippery Slope to Preventive War', *Ethics and International Affairs*, 17 (1), 2003, p. 35.

63 Evan Thomas and Mark Hosenball, 'The Opening Shot: In a Show of Superpower Might, the CIA Kills a Qaeda Operative in Yemen', *Newsweek*, 18 November 2002, p. 48.

64 David Johnstone and David E. Sanger, 'Yemen Killing Based on Rules Set Out by Bush', *New York Times*, 6 November 2002.

65 See Jeffrey Aldicott, 'The Yemen Attack: Illegal Assassination or Lawful Killing?', http://jurist.law.pitt.edu/forum/forumnew68.php, accessed 14 September 2007.

66 Cited by Mary Ellen O'Connell, 'Re-Leashing the Dogs of War', *American Journal of*

International Law, 97 (2), 2003, p. 454.

67 Cited by John J. Lumpkin, 'Administration Says that Bush Has, in Effect, a License to Kill', *St Louis Post Dispatch*, 4 December 2002, p. A12.

68 O'Connell, 'Re-Leashing the Dogs of War', p. 454.

69 Cited by Walter Pincus, 'Missile Strike Carried Out with Yemeni Cooperation: Official Says Operation Authorized Under Bush Finding', *Washington Post*, 6 November 2002, p. A12.

70 John J. Lumpkin, 'US Kills Senior Al Qaeda Leader in Yemen with Missile Strike', Associated Press, 5 November 2002.

71 See Michael Byers, 'Terrorism, the Use of Force and International Law After 11 September', *International and Comparative Law Quarterly*, 51 (2), 2002, pp. 403–4.

72 Human Rights Watch Report Annual Report, *Yemen*, 1993, www.hrw.org/reports/1993/WR93/NEW-1, accessed 17 February 2005.

73 Cited by Pincus, 'Missile Strike', p. A12.

74 Aldicott, 'The Yemen Attack'.

75 Laurie Calhoun, 'The Strange Case of Summary Execution by Predator Drone', *Peace Review*, 15 (2), 2003, pp. 209–14.

76 Asa Kasher, *Military Ethics* (Tel Aviv: Ministry of Defence Press, 1996).

77 Amnesty International, 'Yemen/USA: Government Must Not Sanction Extra-Judicial Executions', http://web.a.mnesty.org/library/Index/engAMR511682002/Open, accessed 14 February 2004.

78 Joanne K. Lekea, 'Missile Strike Carried Out with Yemeni Cooperation – The War Against Terrorism: A Different Type of War?', *Journal of Military Ethics*, 2 (3), 2003, p. 232.

79 Thomas and Hosenball, 'The Opening Shot', p. 48.

80 Calhoun, 'The Strange Case', p. 209.

81 See Sean D. Murphy, 'Use of Military Force to Disarm Iraq', *American Journal of International Law*, 97 (2), 2003, pp. 427–8.

82 Cited by Clarke, *Against All Enemies*, p. 266.

83 S/PV.4644, 2002, p. 3.

84 *Observer*, 14 July 2002.

85 Cited by Clarke, *Against All Enemies*, p. 266.

86 Daalder and Lindsay, *America Unbound*, p. 104.

87 George W. Bush, Speech at Cincinnati, 7 October 2002, www.whitehouse.gov/news/releases/2002/10/20021007-8.html, accessed 2 February 2005.

88 Andrew Dorman, 'The United States and the War on Iraq', in Paul Cornish (ed.), *The Conflict in Iraq, 2003* (London: Palgrave Macmillan, 2004), p. 148.

89 S/PV.4701, 5 February 2003, p. 16.

90 Ibid., p. 17.

91 Jeffrey Record, 'Threat, Confusion and Its Penalties', *Survival*, 46 (2), 2004, pp. 51–71.

92 Clarke, *Against All Enemies*, p. 270.

93 Report of a Committee of Privy Councillors, chaired by Lord Butler of Brockwell, *Review of Intelligence on Weapons of Mass Destruction* (London: Her

Majesty's Stationery Office, 14 July 2004), para. 484, p. 120.

94 Ibid., para. 479, p. 119.

95 Ibid., para. 481, p. 119.

96 Ibid., para. 509, p. 128.

97 S/PV.4701, 5 February 2003, pp. 10–15.

98 Charles Duelfer, *Comprehensive Report of the Special Advisor to the Director of Central Intelligence on Iraq's WMD* (Washington, DC: Government Printing Officer, 30 September 2004).

99 S/PV. 4707, 14 February 2003, p. 6.

100 Ibid., p. 20.

101 See John J. Mearsheimer and Stephen Walt, 'An Unnecessary War', *Foreign Policy*, 134, 2003, pp. 50–60.

5 May we torture ticking-bomb terrorists?

1 Jane Mayer, 'Outsourcing Torture: The Secret History of America's "Extraordinary Rendition" Program', *New Yorker*, 14 February 2005.

2 Anthony Lewis, 'Making Torture Legal', *New York Review*, 15 (12), 15 July 2004, p. 4.

3 David Rose, 'How I Entered the Hellish World of Guantánamo Bay', *Observer*, 6 February 2005.

4 Joint Chiefs of Staff, *Joint Doctrine for Detainee Operations*, Joint Publication 3–63, 23 March 2005, paras 1–4.

5 Admiral Albert T. Church III, *Department of Defense Investigation into Allegations of Abuse*, executive summary (at the time of writing only the executive summary is unclassified), 11 March 2005, pp. 6, 9, 10.

6 Ibid., pp. 17–18.

7 Tom Farer, 'US Abuse of Iraqi Detainees at Abu Ghraib Prison', *American Journal of International Law*, 98 (3), 2004, pp. 592–3.

8 Church, *Department of Defense Investigation*, p. 4.

9 For a first-hand account see Antonio Cassese, *Inhuman States: Imprisonment, Detention and Torture in Europe Today* (Cambridge: Polity, 1996), pp. 73–90.

10 Investigation of the 800th Military Police Brigade at http://news.findlaw.com/hdocs/docs/ iraq/tagubarpt.htm. Accessed 14 July 2006. This quote is from part 1, para. 5.

11 Ibid., part 1, para. 10.

12 Attorney General John Ashcroft before the Senate Judiciary Committee, 'Preserving Our Freedoms While Defending Against Terrorism', Hearing Before the Senate Committee on the Judiciary, 107th Congress, 2001. Accessed at www.usdoj.gov/archive/ag/testimony/2001/1206transcriptsenatejudiciary committee.htm on 15 April 2008.

13 Cited by Lewis, 'Making Torture Legal', p. 2.

14 Slavoj Žižek, *Welcome to the Desert of the Real: Five Essays on September 11 and Similar Dates* (London: Verso, 2002), p. 103.

15 Philip Setunga and Nick Cheeseman (eds), *Torture: A Crime Against Humanity* (Hong Kong: Asian Human Rights Commission, 2001).

16 Nigel S. Rodley, *The Treatment of Prisoners Under International Law* (Oxford: Clarendon Press, 1987), p. 45.

17 Jean Pictet (ed.), *The Geneva Conventions of 12 August 1949*

– *Commentary: III Geneva Convention Relative to the Treatment of Prisoners of War* (Geneva: ICRC, 1960), p. 39.

18 Anon, 'Ashcroft Hold Torture Memo', AFP, 9 June 2004. Accessed at www.news24.com/News24/World/Iraq/0,6119,2-10--1460_1539584,00.html on 28 March 2005.

19 Cited by Lewis, 'Making Torture Legal', p. 2.

20 Ibid.

21 This is detailed in Peter Paret, *French Revolutionary Warfare from Indochina to Algeria* (New York: Praeger, 1964).

22 Wuillaume Report, 2 March 1955, Appendix, pp. 169–79. See P. Vidal-Naquet, *Torture: Cancer of Democracy* (Harmondsworth: Penguin Books, 1963), pp. 50–1.

23 See Neil McMaster, 'Torture: From Algiers to Abu Ghraib', *Race & Class*, 46 (2), 2004, p. 9.

24 Edward Compton, *Report of the Enquiry into Allegation Against the Security Forces of Physical Brutality in Northern Ireland Arising out of Events in August 1971* (the Compton Report), (London: HMSO, 1971).

25 Michael O'Boyle, 'Torture and Emergency Powers Under the European Convention on Human Rights: Ireland v. the United Kingdom', *American Journal of International Law*, 71 (4), 1977, pp. 674–706.

26 See David R. Lowry, 'Ill-Treatment, Brutality and Torture: Some Thoughts upon the "Treatment" of Irish Political Prisoners', *De Paul Law Review*, 22 (3), 1972, pp. 553–81.

27 Report of the European Commission of Human Rights, *Ireland v. United Kingdom*, application no. 5310/71, 25 January 1976, cited by O'Boyle, 'Torture and Emergency Powers', p. 695.

28 Malcolm D. Evans and Rod Morgan, *Preventing Torture: A Study of the European Convention for the Prevention of Torture* (Oxford: Oxford University Press, 1998).

29 David Sussman, 'What's Wrong with Torture?', *Philosophy and Public Affairs*, 33 (1), 2005, p. 2.

30 Ibid., p. 4.

31 Ibid., p. 30.

32 This view is put forward by Henry Shue, 'Torture', *Philosophy and Public Affairs*, 7 (2), 1978, pp. 124–43.

33 Ibid., p. 141.

34 Joel Feinberg, *Social Philosophy* (Englewood Cliffs, NJ: Prentice-Hall, 1973), p. 88.

35 See Fritz Allhoff, 'Terrorism and Torture', *International Journal of Applied Philosophy*, 17 (1), 2003, p. 107. Allhoff himself rejects this argument.

36 See Eyal Press, 'In Torture We Trust?', *The Nation*, 31 March 2003, pp. 1–3

37 Cited by Harry Rosenberg, 'Terror and Immigration Law', *The Nation*, 1 December 2003, p. 7.

38 Staff writers, 'US Decries Abuse but Defends Interrogators', *Washington Post*, 26 December 2002, p. A12.

39 Press, 'In Torture We Trust?', p. 2.

40 Richard Posner, 'The Best Offense', *New Republic*, 2 September 2002, p. 28.

41 Landau Commission, *Report of the Commission of Enquiry into the Methods of Investigation of the General Security Service Regarding Hostile Terrorist Activity, Part One* (Jerusalem: Government of Israel, 1987). Hereafter referred to as Landau Commission.

42 Most notoriously, Louis Lambert, an instructor at the national police college. See Louis Lambert, *Traité Théorique et Pratique de Police Judiciaire* (Paris: Chapitne, 1945).

43 See Mika Haritos-Fatouros, *The Psychological Origins of Institutionalized Torture* (London: Routledge, 2003), p. 3.

44 Cited by W. L. Twining and P. E. Twining, 'Bentham on Torture', *Northern Ireland Legal Quarterly*, 24 (3), 1973, p. 347. My discussion of Bentham draws primarily on this article.

45 Rodley, *Treatment of Prisoners*, p. 76.

46 Landau Commission, *Report of the Commission of Enquiry*, para. 2.11.

47 Ibid., paras 2.16, 2.20, 2.28, 2.38, 4.6.

48 Ibid., para. 4.3.

49 Ibid., para. 4.4.

50 Ibid., para. 4.5.

51 Ibid., para. 2.25. The methods were published in the classified second part of the Commission's report, see Evans and Morgan, *Preventing Torture*, p. 44.

52 See Ignatieff, *The Lesser Evil: Political Ethics in an Age of Terror* (Edinburgh: Edinburgh University Press, 2004).

53 Landau Commission, para. 3.15.

54 Ibid., para. 3.16.

55 Ibid., para. 3.16.

56 Evans and Morgan, *Preventing Torture*, p. 51.

57 Ibid., p. 50.

58 Alan M. Dershowitz, *Why Terrorism Works: Understanding the Threat, Responding to the Challenge* (New Haven, CT: Yale University Press, 2002). The following discussion draws from pp. 137–63 unless otherwise stated.

59 Allhoff, 'Terrorism and Torture', p. 111.

60 Michael Walzer, *Just and Unjust Wars: A Moral Argument with Historical Illustrations* (New York: Basic Books, 1977), p. 36.

61 See Evans and Morgan, *Preventing Torture*, p. 47.

62 Dershowitz, *Why Terrorism Works*, p. 137.

63 See Dan Murphy, 'Filipino Police Uncover 1995 Leads to September 11 Plot', *Christian Science Monitor*, 14 February 2002; Richard Owen and Daniel McGary, 'Al Qaeda in Plot to Assassinate Pope', *Times Online*, 11 November 2002; Center for Cooperative Research, 'Context of February 1995', at www.cooperativeresearch.org/context/jsp?item.000293.thirdplot.html accessed on 12 March 2005.

64 Sanford Levinson, 'The Debate on Torture: War Against Virtual States', *Dissent*, summer 2003, pp. 79–90.

65 Dan Coleman, cited by Jane Mayer, 'Outsourcing Torture', *New Yorker*, 14 February 2005, p. 3.

66 Cited in Robin Gedye, 'British Torture Row Envoy Loses Clearance for Uzbekistan Post', *Telegraph*, 12 October 2004.

67 David Rose, 'Revealed: The Full Story of the Guantánamo Britons', *Observer*, 14 March 2004.

68 See Jacques Massu, *La Vraie Bataille d'Alger* (Evreux: Plon, 1972).

69 Cited by MacMaster, 'Torture', p. 9. For an excellent overview see Neil MacMaster, 'The Torture Controversy (1998–2002): Towards a "New History" of the Algerian War?', *Modern and Contemporary France*, 10 (4), 2002, pp. 449–59.

70 Jules Roy, *J'accuse le General Massu* (Paris: Seuil, 1972), p. 44.

71 See Roy, *J'accuse* and General Paris de Bollardière, *Bataille d'Alger, Bataille de l'Homme* (Paris: Desclée de Brouwer, 1972).

72 Christopher W. Tindale, 'The Logic of Torture: A Critical Examination', *Social Theory and Practice*, 22 (3), 1996, pp. 350–1.

73 Alistair Horne, *A Savage War of Peace: Algeria 1954–62* (London: Macmillan, 1987), 2nd edn, p. 204.

74 Jonathan Allen, 'Warrant to Torture? A Critique of Dershowitz and Levinson', *ACDIS Occasional Paper*, January 2005, p. 9.

75 Shue, 'Torture', pp. 141–2. Emphasis in original.

76 Daniel Moeckli, 'The US Supreme Court's "Enemy Combatant Decisions": A "Major Victory for the Rule of Law?"', *Journal of Conflict and Security Law*, 10 (1), 2005, pp. 75–99.

77 Cited by Press, 'In Torture We Trust?', p. 3.

78 Pierre Vidal-Naquet, *Torture: Cancer of Democracy: France and Algeria, 1954–1962*, translated by B. Richard (Harmondsworth: Penguin, 1963).

79 Jacques Soustelle, *Aimée et Souffrante Algérie* (Paris: Plon, 1956), p. 43.

80 Michel Biran, *Deuxiéme Classe en Algérie* (Paris: Perspectives Socialistes, 1961), p. 33.

81 Vidal-Naquet, *Torture: Cancer of Democracy*, pp. 42–4.

82 Cited by Vidal-Naquet, *Torture: Cancer of Democracy*, p. 51.

83 Roger Trinquier, *La Guerre Moderne* (Paris: Table Rond, 1961), pp. 7–121.

84 Cited by Vidal-Naquet, *Torture: Cancer of Democracy*, p. 51.

85 Peter Benenson, *Persecution* (Harmondsworth: Penguin, 1961), pp. 7–28.

86 Vidal-Naquet, *Torture: Cancer of Democracy*, pp. 120–34.

87 *Yearbook of the European Convention on Human Rights – Ireland vs United Kingdom*, pp. 764–6. Emphasis added.

88 See Derek Jinks, 'International Human Rights Law and the War on Terrorism', *Denver Journal of International Law and Policy*, 31 (1), 2003, pp. 101–12.

89 Michael Walzer, *Arguing About War* (New Haven, CT: Yale University Press, 2004), pp. 45–6.

6 What comes next?

1 This is the most common position. See Brian Orend, 'Justice After War', *Ethics and International Affairs*, 16 (1), 2002, pp. 43–56; and Michael Walzer, *Just and Unjust War: A Moral Argument with Historical Illustrations* (New York: Basic Books, 1977), p. 119.

2 Emmerich de Vattel, *The Law of Nations or the Principles of Natural Law Applied to the Con-*

duct and the Affairs of Nations and of Sovereigns, translated by Charles G. Fenwick (Washington, DC: Carnegie Institution of Washington, 1916), Vol. III, p. 344.

3 Orend, 'Justice After War', p. 56.

4 Francisco de Vitoria, 'On the Laws of War' in A. Pagden and J. Lawrence (eds), *Vitoria: Political Writings* (Cambridge: Cambridge University Press, 1991), p. 303.

5 G. H. J. Van Der Molen, *Alberico Gentili and the Development of International Law: His Life, Work and Times*, 2nd revised edition (Leyden: A. W. Sijthoff, 1968), pp. 116–17.

6 Benedict Kingsbury and Adam Roberts, 'Introduction: Grotian Thought in International Relations', in Hedley Bull, Benedict Kingsbury and Adam Roberts (eds), *Hugo Grotius and International Relations* (Oxford: Clarendon Press, 1992), p. 16.

7 Hugo Grotius, *De Jure Belli ac Pacis Libri Tres*, translated by F. W. Kelsey (Washington, DC: Carnegie Council, 1925), p. 172.

8 Ibid., p. 173.

9 Vattel, *Law of Nations*, p. 11.

10 Ibid., p. 3.

11 Ibid., p. 235.

12 Ibid., p. 236.

13 Ibid.

14 Orend, 'Justice After War', p. 47.

15 Jean Pictet, *Commentary on Geneva Conventions of 1949*, vol. IV (Geneva: ICRC, 1958), p. 273.

16 Walzer, *Just and Unjust Wars*, pp. 122–3; Brian Orend, 'Jus Post Bellum', *Journal of Social Philosophy*, 31 (1), 2000, p. 122.

17 Orend, 'Justice After War', p. 45. Emphasis added.

18 Vattel, *Law of Nations*, p. 344.

19 Ian Clark, *Legitimacy in International Society* (Oxford: Oxford University Press, 2005), p. 220.

20 See Alwyn V. Freeman, 'War Crimes by Enemy Nationals Administering Justice in Occupied Territory', *American Journal of International Law*, 41 (3), 1947, p. 581.

21 Geoffrey Best, *War and Law Since 1945* (Oxford: Clarendon Press, 1994).

22 See Raymond T. Yingling and Robert W. Ginnance, 'The Geneva Conventions of 1949', *American Journal of International Law*, 46 (3), 1952, p. 395.

23 The following discussion draws extensively on Ministry of Defence, *Manual of the Law of Armed Conflict* (Oxford: Oxford University Press, 2005). Unless otherwise stated, the following in-text references refer to paragraphs in the manual.

24 Michael Walzer, 'Just and Unjust Occupations', *Dissent*, winter 2004, pp. 61–2.

25 Ibid.

26 Ibid.

27 Ibid.

28 See Michael J. Schuck, 'When the Shooting Stops: Missing Elements in Just War Theory', *The Christian Century*, 26 October 1994.

29 See Paul Rogers, *Iraq and the War on Terror: Twelve Months of Insurgency* (London: I.B. Tauris, 2005).

30 Gary Bass, 'Jus Post Bellum',

Philosophy and Public Affairs, 32 (4), 2004, pp. 384–412.

31 Nicholas J. Wheeler, *Saving Strangers: Humanitarian Intervention in International Society* (Oxford: Oxford University Press, 2000).

32 International Commission on Intervention and State Sovereignty, *The Responsibility to Protect* (Ottawa: ICISS, 2002).

33 Carsten Stahn, 'Jus ad Bellum, Jus in Bello … Jus post Bellum? – Rethinking the Conception of Law in Armed Force', *European Journal of International Law*, 17 (5), 2007, pp. 921–43.

34 See Brad R. Roth, *Government Illegitimacy in International Law* (Oxford: Oxford University Press, 2000), pp. 37–41.

35 See W. Michael Reisman, 'Stopping Wars and Making Peace: Reflections on the Ideology of Conflict Termination in Contemporary World Politics', *Tulane Journal of International and Comparative Law*, 6 (5), 1998.

36 The basic propositions come from Eyal Benvenisti, 'The Security Council and the Law on Occupation: Resolution 1483 in Historical Perspective', *Israel Defence Forces Law Review*, 19 (1), 2003, pp. 23–7.

37 See Eyal Benvenisti, *The International Law of Occupation* (Princeton, NJ: Princeton University Press, 2004), pp. 59–106.

38 Benvenisti, 'The Security Council and the Law', p. 25.

39 Ibid., p. 26.

40 Ibid.

41 Ibid., pp. 25–8.

42 Cited in Best, *Law and War*, p. 118.

43 William Shawcross, 'After Iraq: America and Europe', 2003 Harkness Lecture, King's College London, 27 March 2003.

44 James Traub, *The Best Intentions: Kofi Annan and the UN in an Era of American Power* (New York: Farar, Strauss and Giroux, 2006).

45 A/56/875–S/2002/278, 18 March 2002.

46 Alex J. Bellamy and Paul D. Williams, 'Contemporary Peace Operations: Four Challenges for the Brahimi Paradigm', *Yearbook of Peace Operations*, 11, 2007, pp. 1–28.

47 Simon Chesterman, *You, the People: The United Nations, Transitional Administration and Statebuilding* (Oxford: Oxford University Press, 2005); ibid.

48 Traub, *Best Intentions*, p. 164.

49 RAND, *America's Role in Nation-Building* (Santa Monica, CA: RAND, 2007).

50 International Crisis Group, 'After Baker-Hamilton: What to Do in Iraq', Middle East Report No. 60, 19 December 2006, p. 1.

51 Gareth Evans, 'The Unfinished Responsibility to Protect Agenda: Europe's Role', speech given to the EPC/IPPR/Oxfam policy dialogue meeting, 5 July 2007.

Index